D1488167

THE BEST
BURLESQUE
SKETCHES

The Street Drop

THE BEST BURLESQUE SKETCHES

Adapted by
Ralph Allen

for
Sugar Babies

and other Entertainments

Illustrated by
Peter Larkin

Foreword by
Dick Martin

With annotations and a brief
essay on the history of Burlesque

APPLAUSE
THEATRE ❦ BOOKS

To the Memory of
Billy Hagan
Maxie Furman
Bert Carr
Billy Foster

Condemned to hope's delusive mine,
As on we toil from day to day,
By sudden blasts or slow decline,
Our social comforts drop away.

— Samuel Johnson

The social comforts of my youth included weekly matinees at the Troc Burlesque Theatre in Philadelphia where I met the comedians to whom I dedicate this collection. They were already old men when I first saw them perform—thirty-five or forty years ago. They cheered me when I was young; they inspired me in my middle age. The memory of their wit sustains me now and finds its way onto every page of this book.

These Harlequins of the Tenderloin were the most accomplished low comedians of their generation. I am proud to say that they were also my friends.

I am grateful to Peter Larkin, the distinguished Broadway designer, whose cartoons and drawings grace this volume. Obviously, Mr. Larkin had a misspent youth not unlike my own. While I was visiting the Troc in Philadelphia, he was haunting the Old Howard in Boston. Neither of us seems to be the worse for it.

I also owe thanks to Glenn Young of Applause, who commissioned this collection, and to Andrew Pontious, his talented editor, who provided expert advice and help.

As she has for many years, Harriet Nichols gave me the benefit of her wise counsel.

An Applause Original
The Best Burlesque Sketches
Copyright 1995 by Ralph Allen.

All rights, including the right to perform these adapted sketches, are strictly reserved.

All inquiries regarding publication rights including anthology and translation should be addressed to: Rights Dept., Applause Books, 211 W. 71st St. New York, NY 10023.

The scenes beginning on pp. 1, 50, 71, 79, 103, 104, 145, 151, 172, 181, 186, 188, 189, 197 and 199 (copyright 1979 by Ralph Allen) are from the revue *Sugar Babies* and may not be performed independently of that production. Stock and amateur theatres who wish to present this revue should apply to Samuel French, Inc., 45 West 25th Street, New York, NY 10010.

The scene beginning on p. 111 (copyright 1984 by Ralph Allen) is from the revue *Diamonds*. Producers seeking permission to perform *Diamonds* should also apply to Samuel French at the above address.

The scenes on pp. 14, 139 and 183 (copyright 1986 by Ralph Allen and David Campbell) are from the musical play *Honky Tonk Nights* (music by Michael Valenti). For permission to perform this play, write to: Performing Rights Division, Applause Books, 211 West 71st Street, New York, NY 10023.

All the other scenes (copyright 1994 by Ralph Allen) are not part of a revue or musical. Inquiries concerning performance rights should be addressed to: Performing Rights Division, Applause Books, at the above address.

Library of Congress Cataloging-in-Publication Data

Allen, Ralph G.
    The best burlesque sketches / adapted by Ralph Allen for Sugar Babies and other entertainments ; illustrated by Peter Larkin ; introduction by Dick Martin.
    p. cm.
    "With annotations and a brief essay on the history of burlesque."
    "An Applause original."
    ISBN 1-55783-189-0
    I. Burlesques. I. Title.
PN6231.B84A45   1994
812'.54--dc20   94-34272
                                                  CIP

British Library Cataloging-in-Publication Data

A catalogue record for this book is available from the British Library.

Applause Books
211 West 71st Street
New York, NY 10023
Phone (212) 496-7511
Fax: (212) 721-2856
First Applause Printing 1995

Printed in Canada

406 Vale Road
Tonbridge Kent TN9 1XR
Phone 073 235-7755
Fax 073 207-7219

TABLE OF CONTENTS

APPENDIX:

LIST OF ILLUSTRATIONS
BY PETER LARKIN

FOREWORD

by Dick Martin

FOREWORD

I was a little young to be in Burlesque but not too young to enjoy it. I was raised in Detroit where we had three Burlesque houses: the National, the Gaiety, and the Empress.

I'm sure I went to see the ladies take their clothes off, but I ended up falling in love with the comedy—the sketches performed by guys like Billy "Zoot" Reed, West and Lexing, and Scurvy Miller.

Burlesque was as much attitude as material, and years later when I teamed up with Dan Rowan and started playing clubs, I was amazed at how much Burlesque crept into our act and every other act working the clubs.

Burlesque was always done on a proscenium stage. As a result the comic and the straight man both faced the audience and did their routine.

It wasn't until Dean Martin teamed up with Jerry Lewis that a comic and straight man faced each other. Because they were working night clubs they were able to develop a relationship. In Dean's and Jerry's case it was big brother-little brother. With Dan and me it was almost professor-student with my misunderstanding, or as they would say in Burlesque, misconstruing him.

We did a lot of Burlesque on *Rowan and Martin's Laugh In*. Sammy Davis brought back Pigmeat's "Here Comes The Judge." We did all sorts of crossovers.

This book is one of the funniest I've ever read, and it brought back many fond memories.

Dick Martin
Malibu, California
August 1994

BURLESQUE REMEMBERED

BURLESQUE REMEMBERED*

by Ralph Allen

Sad to say there is no native American form of drama—in the sense of a realized literary style uniquely reflective of the spirit of the New World. Our culture, like that of all colonial peoples, was borrowed—and borrowed at a time when the dramatic impulse in Europe was fitful, weak and sentimental. "Our hybrid drama," as Montrose Moses notes in an essay promoting folk theatre (1931), "has touched the soil as lightly as we touch it, when by train we roll from one state to another."

True enough. From *The Contrast* to last year's musical, our plays mostly are second-hand imitations of European originals. Even the exciting modernist experiments at the end of the last century reached us in a diluted form. Instead of Shaw, we had Bronson Howard; instead of Ibsen, James A. Hearn; instead of *A Dream Play*, *The Hairy Ape*.

A patriotic and serious-minded critic like Moses would seem to have every cause for complaint.

2

Moses, like most of us, views the history of the theatre as the history of its official literature: *Hamlet* and *King Lear* not "Silly Simpkin's Jig," *Cato* and *The Conscious Lovers* not Rich's pantomimes, *The Iceman Cometh* not "Dr. Kronkite." Yet, often the illegitimate entertainments speak more directly to the tastes and enthusiasms of their audience than do the so-called higher forms.

Moses, like Captain Ahab, lacks "the low-enjoying power." Therefore, you will find no mention in his essay of a highly developed and immensely popular "folk theatre" which was flourishing even as he was decrying our lack of native dramatic forms. The folk theatre in question was the Burlesque show. Like most folk art, it was proletarian in spirit. And like the pantomimes of Rich, it was more firmly rooted in the life of its public than the more pretentious alternative forms, including the romantic verse tragedies, the come-

---

*Some of the observations in this preface first appeared in my essay "Our Native Theatre" in Henry B. Williams, editor, *The American Theatre, A Sum of Its Parts*, Samuel French, Inc., New York , 1971. Reprinted by permission.

dies of manners and the sentimental well-made plays which filled the stages of New York year after year.

In recent years theatre scholars have begun to take an interest in Burlesque. My revue, *Sugar Babies*, helped create that interest and also profited from it. But after years of neglect the historians are overpraising what they previously ignored. Regretfully, much folk art is bad art, and Burlesque, spawned in the slums of our cities, was often tasteless and dull. *Sugar Babies*, therefore, could not succeed as an antiquarian exercise, nor for that matter could this anthology.

The sketches (and the production numbers) had to be adapted, and, dare I say it, improved. For *Sugar Babies* was not to be a slavish recreation of a Mutual era production—but a quintessential Burlesque show—a show of shows as I had played it so often in the theatre of my mind. For in a theatre of the mind, nothing disappoints. The dancing women are always beautiful and the comics droll and witty—which was not always the case at the Casino, Pittsburgh; the Roxy, Cleveland or the Gayety, Baltimore.

3

Where did the materials for this quintessential show come from?

The origins of the American Burlesque show can be traced to the subliterary entertainments of the nineteenth-century—to the blackface comic turns of Tom "Jim Crow" Rice, to the minstrel shows that evolved from those turns, to the crosstalk, semi-improvisational dialogues of the Western honky-tonks and to the knockabout farces of the dime museums and variety halls.

Apologists for Burlesque trace its beginnings to much older and more reputable forms—the comedies of Aristophanes, for instance, and *commedia dell'arte*. In actual fact Burlesque is rooted in native not alien soil, even if certain aspects of it were seeded from abroad.

Thus, an English show, *Lydia Thompson and Her London Blondes*, which in 1869 had a scandalous success in New York, is sometimes thought to be the first Burlesque show that deserves to be called by that name. But Lydia did a burlesque (with a small "b") of classical legends in the style made popular in London by H. J. Byrom. As in English pantomime, the principal boys were played by girls in tights. During an era considerably less frank than our own, the Blondes caused a sensation both on and off the stage. Lydia, for example, was a very forthright woman. In Chicago she acted out the fantasy of many a slighted actor, when she publicly horsewhipped the leading newspaper critic of the city because he had made the painful mistake of belittling her performance in print.

While Lydia's company had many imitators, the English model was not the most congenial to American sensibilities. A more important influence was the honky-tonk, a curious 19th-century institution—part beer hall, part brothel—which featured variety entertainments of the most vulgar sort. The honky-tonk actors did individual turns in a format similar to Vaudeville, then together performed a light-hearted afterpiece. The audiences in the honky-tonks were unsophisticated; the atmosphere was one of rough sodden conviviality.

At places like Bottle Koenig's in San Francisco or the Haymarket in Kansas City, a performer frequently was called on to play seven or eight shows a night. His sketches were largely improvised. The dialogue was seldom written down, and the actor depended for his appeal on his own wit and his own business rather than on the borrowed words of a professional writer.

While the honky-tonk supplied the tone and characteristic atmosphere of Burlesque, still another native form of entertainment, the minstrel show, gave producers the structure into which the basic elements of the performance could be fitted. The minstrel show, which William Dean Howells called "the only genuinely indigenous form of American drama," is a piece of folk entertainment which has no relationship to the folk whose life and character it is supposed to depict. Created by white men for white men, the stock character of the blackfaced comic, his complexion not the product of heredity, but of burnt cork, represents our forefathers' simplistic vision of the plantation Negro—carefree, cunning, greedy and perpetually optimistic. Tambo and Bones (as the minstrel clowns were called) are synthetic characters surely, but unusually attractive ones, as the continued success of minstrel shows during the second half of the last century clearly indicates.

The man who combined the atmosphere of the honky-tonk with the patterns of the minstrel shows was M. J. Leavitt, the Ziegfeld of the Tenderloin,* who began his long and profitable career as a producer in 1870. Leavitt borrowed without much alteration the stock format used by E. P. Christy and others in fashioning their blackfaced shows. Like Christy and his many imitators, Leavitt presented a three-part performance: the first, a series of comic questions and answers interspersed with musical interludes and climaxed by a walk-around or cakewalk; the second, an olio of specialty acts, and the third, a farcical afterpiece, sometimes a burlesque of a legitimate play. The most novel feature of Leavitt's productions (following Lydia Thompson) was the substitution of attractive women for the traditional blackfaced clowns, but subsequent Burlesque producers restored the comedians to a central role in the performance.

---

*Or should I call Ziegfeld the Leavitt of Broadway?

The minstrel influence remained dominant in Burlesque until the turn of the century. Indeed, the relationship of the minstrel interlocutor (the whitefaced pretentious asker of questions) to the end men (the blackfaced suppliers of comic answers) became the basis of most of the comic scenes in Burlesque. The interlocutor evolved into the straight man (or feeder) and the end men, their black make-up transmuted into putty nose and clown white, became the cunning tramps who appeared in various guises in every Burlesque performance from the days of W. C. Fields to Jackie Gleason.

Leavitt gave Burlesque respectability, taking it out of the saloons and putting it into theatres. His company, *The Rentz-Santley Show*, brought this kind of entertainment to every corner of America. Imitators were legion.

The bawdy humor of these performances was successful immediately with audiences who never would have compromised their reputations by attending a honky-tonk. Actually "bawdy" is not the right adjective. Burlesque was always franker in its treatment of sex than the legitimate theatre of its period, but Leavitt's extravaganzas were tame indeed by comparison to current Broadway fare.

By the turn of the century, the comedian was the unquestioned star of the show, a position he did not relinquish until the advent of strip tease in the early 1930's. The golden age of Burlesque began in 1905 with the organization by Samuel Scribner of the Columbia Circuit. (A circuit or wheel was an association of theatre owners all using on a rotating basis the same schedule of shows.) The number of theatres on the Columbia Wheel varied from year to year, but during some seasons 40 weeks of work were guaranteed to each franchised company. The rival wheel in 1905 was the Empire (or Western) Circuit. In the 1920's the position of Columbia was challenged by the Mutual Burlesque Association, organized by I. Herk. Mutual developed a new formula, which consisted of a fast alternation of scenes and numbers more or less in the style of a modern revue. Columbia refused to change its style and continued to use the three-part traditional structure inherited from the minstrels. Mutual Burlesque shows were more risqué than the offerings on the older circuit.

Columbia prided itself on providing clean entertainments suitable for everyone. Scribner, a family man who took his religion seriously, employed a network of censors to restrain those comedians who might be tempted to go beyond the allowable limits of decency in order to steal an extra laugh. Herk and his associates were more permissive, and eventually that permissiveness won the day. Columbia was forced out of business. In the next decade, Mutual itself collapsed, but a number of theatre owners formed a new circuit under the management of Izzy Hirst. The Hirst Circuit dominated the business for more than 25 years and survived even the banning of Burlesque in

Straight and Comic

New York in 1942. During this period, the circuit had competition from theatres which played stock Burlesque and from tabloid shows (*i.e.*, hour-length road shows designed for the saloon trade and particularly popular in the South).

The most famous of the many stock Burlesque houses in the '30's were those operated by the Minsky family. The Minskys are widely credited with having ruined Burlesque by substituting erotic stimulation for humor and encouraging pornographic performances. Actually these shrewd producers were simply responding to the triple shock that the variety business suffered in 1929. In that fateful year the stock market crashed, and sound movies made an ominous appearance. Shortly thereafter, radio brought free entertainment into American homes for the first time. The combination of tight money and new competition killed the big Vaudeville circuits, and the Minsky organization only kept Burlesque alive by offering the kind of erotic performances that neither movies nor radio could or would provide. In the short run the policy was profitable, but in the long term it led to the persecution of Burlesque by municipal authorities and its eventual extinction as a comic entertainment.

By 1962 the handwriting was on the wall. Realizing that the stock houses and the shrunken circuits would not survive the decade, I began to collect Burlesque material. With the help of some of the still active comics, I amassed a library of 1,800 Burlesque scenes. At first I thought I would write a critical study of them. But folk comedy is best preserved in performance, and even in the 1960's, I began to hope that the fruits of my research would be not just a monograph, but a production.

In 1964 I created my first Burlesque show, *The Naughty Nifties* (Fred Burleigh's title), for the Pittsburgh Playhouse. As in the case of *Sugar Babies* fifteen years later, the sketches in the Pittsburgh show were not verbatim transcriptions of the stock scenes played by Columbia and Mutual Wheel comedians. Our show was no historical exercise, but an attempt to capture the cheerful spirit of the jokes of a vanished era.

The Naughty Nifties, which featured Bert Carr, had an enormous success and was extended twice after an initial sold-out run. I brought Carr to the University and presented a second Burlesque show the following year. But other interests soon distracted me, and a little later I went to Western Canada to run a classical theatre company on a university campus. Preoccupied with Shakespeare, Webster, Molière and Lope de Vega, I had no time to pursue my practical research into popular comedy.

In fact, I did not think about Burlesque again until 1976. By then I was back in the United States, teaching at the University of Tennessee, and supervising, with the late Anthony Quayle, another college-based professional repertory theatre. As the Bicentennial celebrations approached, it suddenly occurred to me that our company had never performed an American piece, and that the occasion demanded one. Rather than mount another tepid revival of O'Neill, Williams or Miller, I turned again to our most vital form of popular entertainment.

With a cast including Joe E. Ross, Jimmy Matthews, Richard Galuppi, Bernie Engel and Donna King, *The New Majestic Follies and Lyceum Gardens Revue* opened at the Clarence Brown Theatre in October 1976, and I immediately recognized that the show had a commercial future. Unfortunately, I could not persuade any New York producers to come to Knoxville to see it.

Still, I persisted. In 1977 the American Society for Theatre Research sponsored a conference at Lincoln Center on the history of popular entertainments. Papers were commissioned on minstrel shows, theme parks, vaudeville, popular melodramas and spectacles. I was invited to speak about Burlesque.

I must admit to a certain low cunning here. Instead of delivering a dry historical paper, I decided to describe the quintessential Burlesque show I had presented at Knoxville with the jokes intact. I called my presentation "At My Mother's Knee and Other Low Joints," and confident of my ability to make my academic audience laugh, I invited Harry Rigby, the Broadway producer, to attend the conference. My strategy had its desired effect. "We ought to do a show like that," he said. Whereupon, I handed him my script.

Rigby and I then began a two-year effort to get the show produced. I chose Mickey Rooney for the lead, and he took a lot of convincing. Harry pursued Ann Miller who reluctantly said yes. Ernest Flatt came aboard, and he brought Arthur Malvin. Our confidence proved justified. *Sugar Babies* played almost four years on Broadway, spawned three national companies and productions in Australia, England and the American gambling casinos. Obviously, the style we were recreating had not lost its power to delight and amuse.

4

This book contains fifty-five Burlesque bits, some of them short dramatized jokes and some fully developed scenes lasting in performance from eight to twelve minutes. Except for the scripts in the Appendix, all these bits have been adapted and altered from the originals to fit the demands of *Sugar Babies*, *Honky Tonk Nights* and other Broadway and off-Broadway shows.

I have excellent authority for altering these scenes. The comedians themselves often made changes in the received material. A certain amount of adaptation and spontaneous improvisation was permitted in a bit, provided that the premise was not entirely lost. The text was like the *sogetto* of the *commedia dell'arte*. It was an outline of the action, a frame into which the comic inserted his own pieces of business (his *lazzi*, if you will) and some of his stock speeches (his *concetti*). What comics like Billy Hagan did for themselves, I did for Mickey Rooney and Ann Miller, and later for Eddie Bracken, Rip Taylor, Cleavon Little and the rest.

Rooney, whose father was a famous Burlesque comic, knew instinctively the tone and style of this kind of humor. He avoided even the suggestion of sentimentality. He made the right choices. The clown in Burlesque was never a pathetic figure. He was not in any sense the tearful tramp of Chaplin. In most bits he is represented as a child of nature—the slave of stimulus and response. A girl with obvious attractions appears. He is obviously attracted. The straight man, in attempting to demonstrate love-making techniques to the comic starts massaging the latter's stomach, whereupon the comic forgets about the girl and kisses the straight man. The Burlesque show tramp represents man stripped of his inhibitions, of restraints of all kinds—free of moral pretense, innocent of education and, above all, lazy and selfish. He frequently appears to be a victim, but never a pathetic one, because in nine bits out of ten he blunders at the end into some kind of dubious success. Of course, on some occasions he does fail. But even when the comic is left with egg in his hat or pie on his face, the audience feels no pity for him because it senses his infinite resilience.

Slaves of Stimulus and Response

This quality, this resilience, he shares with another great low comedian, Arlecchino—I mean the Arlecchino of Dominique not the softer version that John Rich played. Mickey Rooney's character was a grotesque zany whose low animal shrewdness was paradoxically balanced by a naive, but never innocent predisposition to commit awkward blunders.

In so doing, Mickey was perfectly true to the spirit of the material. We root for the comic not the straight man in the bloodless and fantastic battles of the Burlesque bit, but ours is a partisanship in which the emotions definitely are not engaged. We want him (the comic) to win because all of us (with part of our minds at least) need to see authority toppled. The Burlesque show appeals to our inner passion for anarchy. It appeals also to our desire to renounce the painful effort of intelligence and behave as creatures of instinct not of will.

In addressing itself to all these temporary antisocial childlike inclinations, this most American of all entertainments dramatized the wish-fulfillment fantasies of a society that thought and still thinks of itself as classless. But the celebration of disorder was contained in an orderly, predictable, indeed, highly conventional structure. As a result, anarchy seemed always exhilarating, never threatening.

5

The structure of a typical Burlesque scene is a critique of common sense. And a critique also of sentiment. Pathos, of course, is another form of moral restraint, and Burlesque delighted in making fun of it.

In fact, much of the humor in the bits is dependent upon the reversal of an expected sentimental response. In the "Minding Baby" skit, for example, the comic enters wheeling a baby carriage, and the squawling voice of a child is heard. The comedian takes up a beer bottle and starts pounding the unseen child. "That will teach the little sucker," the comic says, pleased with himself, whereupon the unseen baby urinates in his face.

As we might expect, scatological humor is plentiful in Burlesque. The comedian, frightened of an imaginary ghost in the "Haunted House," defecates in his pants, an age-old manner of expressing comic fear, as any reader of *Aristophanes* will recall. Anything goes in Burlesque. Even mental illness (in bits like "Crazy House") and physical deformity (in scenes like "The Music Master") are not exempt from derisive laughter. The grotesque elements in Burlesque are another reminder of the similarities between this American entertainment and the Renaissance *commedia*. The hunchback of Pulcinella, the stooped, hen-like, nervous walk of Pantalone, the rat-like eyes and wart-ridden mask of Arlecchino—these distortions are mirrored certainly in the painted leer and the distorted features of the putty-nosed, baggy-pants comic of the Mutual era. The early prints of the androgynous Arlecchino enduring the pangs of labor and giving birth to a deformed image of himself are reflected in the hundreds of sodomitical situations in Burlesque. Equally grotesque are the constant pairings of ill-matched lovers, those incongruous marriages of ancient lechery and simpering false virginity.

There is no question that these grotesque jokes are tasteless, especially out of context. Burlesque was tasteless, intentionally so. It delighted in shocking our sensibilities. However, the sexual humor in these entertainments was never designed as an aphrodisiac. There is nothing sentimental or voluptuous in these bits, nothing in the scenes which reflects the voyeuristic pleasures of latter-day strip tease. The action of most Burlesque bits is an almost mechanical parody of sexual desire, and its effect is similar to the one described by Bergson in the section of his essay which deals with the interchangeability of objects and persons as a source of laughter. Indeed, the image of the cunning tramp—naive and brutal—reminds us of the much more self-conscious figures in the Ubu plays of Bergson's disciple, Jarry. The disreputable character that Billy Hagan played in these scenes and that Mickey recreated in *Sugar Babies* is an archetypical image of man's eternal imbecility—indefatigable, enduring.

The comparison with Jarry and Jarry's imitators, Ionesco and Albee, is not inappropriate. It is to the absurdist comedies that we must look for an equivalent of the unsentimental style of the typical Burlesque sketch. But the differences between *The American Dream* and "The Egg in the Hat" are as significant as their similarities. Despite its grotesqueries, despite its attack on sentiment, its defiance of authority, its celebration of freedom, Burlesque was never a comedy of despair. It was never moralistic, never bitter, never passionately critical of human absurdity.

The defeat of the fast-talking straight man by the cunning man of instinct was a perpetual and easily recognized symbol of the durability of man—a tribute to his tenacity, if not to his intelligence or selflessness. This curiously attractive image of human nature is one of the great achievements of our popular culture. Let us hope that it endures.

Note: The scenes that follow have two titles. The ones in parentheses are the traditional names the comics used to identify the sketches. Often these names give away the punch line of the scene. Therefore, I have included some jokey, but less revealing titles for use on programs and enunciators.

SCENES

That lady dropped her pocketbook.

Burlesque sketches belong to one of two basic categories—flirtation scenes and body scenes.

A flirtation scene is a short single-joke situation played in front of a downstage drop by a comic, the straight man and a talking woman or two. (Burlesque never employed actresses, just talking women and dancing women.)

In a typical flirtation scene, the straight man (an immaculately dressed authority figure) has a secret method for succeeding with women. He may own a manual of seduction ("The Love Book") or a magic peanut which emits stimulating vapors ("The Tweeter, or King Tut's Nut"). Or he may simply be such a smooth talker that women find him irresistible ("The Ukulele Scene"). He promises to teach his technique to the comic whose approaches to the opposite sex have not been notably successful:

COMIC Do you smoke?
GIRL I don't know. I never get that hot.
   ("Poppy Poppy" as played by Billy Fields)

COMIC I beg your pardon.
GIRL What the hell are you begging for? You're old enough to ask for it.
   ("The Ukulele" as played by Billy Hagan)

Habitués of Burlesque, and (as the candy butcher might say) sons of habitués, know these jokes, but knowledge in no way diminishes pleasure. Bergson notwithstanding, surprise is not one of the essentials of Burlesque humor. Patrons enjoyed knowing that no new ground would be broken. Like Aristotle, they preferred irony to suspense.

In most flirtation scenes, the comic eventually blunders into some kind of dubious success to the consternation of his glibber partner.

Some of these scenes are short and simple; others are more elaborate. My personal favorite is "Meet Me Round the Corner." This sketch about a quartet of friends who promise to stay together, but who succumb one by one to feminine temptation, was played for fifty years on the Columbia and Mutual Circuits. There is no known source for the scene, and it possibly developed improvisationally out of rehearsal situations. Many variations exist, but I based my version (for Mickey Rooney) on the classic one of Billy Hagan, shortening it somewhat and adding some jokes from other sources. The original punch of this sketch was considered too vulgar by Harry Rigby and Terry Kramer, our producers. So I watered it down in performance. I've restored the original ending, however, confident that the sophisticated readers of this book will not be shocked or offended.

FLIRTATIONS
("Meet Me Round the Corner")

ORCHESTRA plays a signature tune; lights up on street scene in one. 2ND COMIC enters right. JUVENILE enters left. THEY meet, ad lib greetings at center.

JUVENILE Well, _____.*

2ND COMIC Well, _____.

JUVENILE What have you been doing these days?

2ND COMIC I've been working as a pilot in a livery stable.

JUVENILE A pilot in a livery stable?

2ND COMIC Yeah. I pile it here. I pile it there.

JUVENILE Well, you sound as if you could use some money. You'd better join our quartet.

(STRAIGHT enters right.)

STRAIGHT Hi, boys. Is this where the quartet is going to rehearse?

JUVENILE That's right. But there's only three of us.

STRAIGHT *(gesturing toward proscenium)* Well, don't worry, boys, I've asked a friend of mine to join us, a man of culture and refinement. And here he comes now.

(Enter 1ST COMIC in black pants and jacket. A dickey and black tie only partially conceal his red underwear. HE is very disheveled and looks as if HE has been thrown on the stage.)

1ST COMIC *(in wings)* I still don't think it was worth five dollars. *(big ad lib greeting)*

JUVENILE Hi, _____. It's good to see you. What have you been doing these days?

---

*Use the real name of performer.

2

1ST COMIC I've been working at a ladies' bloomer factory.

JUVENILE Is it a good job?

1ST COMIC Yeah, I pull down fifty a week.

STRAIGHT Well, pal, they need a quartet down at the Gaiety Theatre. Can you sing?

1ST COMIC Sure. I used to sing in a queer.

STRAIGHT No, no. You mean a choir.

1ST COMIC It was a queer choir.

STRAIGHT A queer choir?

1ST COMIC Yes, we weren't even sure about the man who played the organ.

STRAIGHT What do you mean?

1ST COMIC He played nothing but hymns.

STRAIGHT What was your best singing performance?

1ST COMIC Oh, I used to sing in the opera. *(HE begins to sing an aria.)*

STRAIGHT What opera is that?

1ST COMIC Madame Caterpillar.

STRAIGHT No, you mean Madame Butterfly.

1ST COMIC Well, I knew her before she was out of the cocoon.

STRAIGHT Come on, boys, we'd better rehearse. What song shall we sing?

2ND COMIC How about that old sailors' song?

STRAIGHT What song is that?

2ND COMIC "SHE WAS ONLY A FISHERMAN'S DAUGHTER, BUT WHEN I SHOWED HER MY ROD SHE REELED."

STRAIGHT I've got a better idea. We'll sing out of these books. *(HE passes out songbooks.)* But, first, we have to have a name for the quartet.

JUVENILE How about the Avon Comedy Four?

STRAIGHT Aw, no. That's too old-fashioned. We need something mellifluous, something that will make the audience think of gentle zephyrs wafting over fields of new-mown hay. Something with an air about it.

2ND COMIC How about the Shedhouse Quartet?

1ST COMIC That does have an air about it.

3

The Shedhouse Quartet

JUVENILE What page are we gonna sing on?

STRAIGHT Sing on page fourteen.

2ND COMIC There's no page fourteen in my book.

1ST COMIC Sing on page seven twice. *(2ND COMIC sings a few bars of an aria. HE hits 2ND COMIC with his songbook.)* Just a minute. What are you singing?

2ND COMIC Paganini.

1ST COMIC Whatya mean, Paganini? Let me see that.

2ND COMIC See, it says right there, Paganini. *(shows 1ST COMIC the book)*

1ST COMIC Paganini. You idiot. That says page nine.

STRAIGHT Well, we've to to sing something. Have you any suggestions, _____?

2ND COMIC "I WANT A GIRL."

1ST COMIC Let's sing first.

2ND COMIC No. "I WANT A GIRL."

1ST COMIC We don't want to know your personal problems.

JUVENILE I think he means, "I WANT A GIRL JUST LIKE THE GIRL THAT MARRIED DEAR OLD DAD."

STRAIGHT That's it. That's good.

1ST COMIC Ladies and gentlemen, you will now be entertained by the Shedhouse Quartet.

> *(HE winces at the name. A triangle sounds, giving them the note. THEY sing, accompanied by the ORCHESTRA.)*

ALL. I WANT A GIRL
  JUST LIKE THE GIRL
  THAT MARRIED DEAR OLD DAD.
  SHE WAS A PEARL
  AND THE ONLY GIRL...

> *(On "SHE WAS A PEARL," the 1ST GIRL enters. SHE is dressed like a tart. SHE walks, backed by the DRUMMER, to the R. proscenium. As SHE passes JUVENILE, SHE drops her purse at his feet. While waiting for him to pick up the purse, SHE stands motionless except for some agitation of the hips. The MEN, of course, trail off in their song.)*

JUVENILE Wait a minute, boys. That lady dropped her pocketbook,

5

Just for that, honey, you can...

and me, being a Southern gentleman, I shall pick it up and return it to her. *(HE does so.)* Pardon me, lady, you dropped your pocketbook.

1ST GIRL Oh, thank you. *(SHE opens the purse, then shuts it fast.)* And I can see that all my money is still here. Well, just for that, honey, you can...

> MEET ME ROUND THE CORNER
> IN A HALF AN HOUR;
> MEET ME ROUND THE CORNER
> IN A HALF AN HOUR;
> MEET ME ROUND THE CORNER
> IN—A—HALF—AN—HOUR.

(During this recitation, SHE does a jazzy box step with a pelvic thrust, grinding on the last line and bumping on the last word. A follow spot narrows on her pelvis. When SHE bumps, the spot leaves her pelvis, arches across the street drop and goes out at L. proscenium. Appropriate

6

percussion accompanies this movement of light. 1ST COMIC starts to howl lustfully. HE sounds as if HE were in pain.)

STRAIGHT Did she thrill you, _____?

1ST COMIC No, I just got my suspenders caught in my jockey shorts.

JUVENILE *(at R. proscenium, turns to others)* Boys, did you see what she said?

1ST COMIC No. What did she say?

JUVENILE *(same business as 1ST GIRL)* She...said...that...I...could...
MEET HER ROUND THE CORNER
IN A HALF AN HOUR;
MEET HER ROUND THE CORNER
IN A HALF AN HOUR;
MEET HER ROUND THE CORNER
IN...A...HALF...AN...HOUR.

(JUVENILE grinds, bumps, exits. Spotlight hits 2ND COMIC. HE reacts.)

2ND COMIC *(after pause, starts R.)* I think I'll take him.

She said that I could...

7

STRAIGHT No, you don't, _____. *(STRAIGHT grabs 2ND COMIC by the seat of his pants.)*

2ND COMIC Hey, you're choking me.

1ST COMIC Ladies and gentlemen, you will now be entertained by the Shedhouse Trio.

> *(HE winces. The triangle again. ALL sing as before. On the same cue [i.e., "SHE WAS A PEARL"], 2ND GIRL enters, repeats the earlier business, only this time SHE drops a pocketbook with a brick in it. It hits 2ND COMIC's foot. HE yelps and pushes it to STRAIGHT.)*

STRAIGHT That lady dropped her pocketbook.

2ND COMIC She must have had a busy night.

STRAIGHT Well, me being a Southern gentleman, I will pick it up and return it to her. *(HE does so.)* Pardon me, miss, you dropped your pocketbook.

2ND GIRL Thank you, sir, and I can see that all my money is still there. Just for that, you can...

> MEET ME ROUND THE CORNER, etc.

> *(Repeated three times as before, leading to grind, bump and exit. As SHE grinds, STRAIGHT crouches like a catcher. The spot leaves her pelvis. HE catches it, throws it in the air. The spot circles around the auditorium as the COMEDIANS run around like outfielders under a pop fly. Finally, 2ND COMIC catches it in his baggy pants.)*

The Shedhouse Brothers

...me being a Southern gentleman...

2ND COMIC *(with a big smile)* I got it.

1ST COMIC It'll be safe down there.

    STRAIGHT *(now at L. proscenium)* Hey, boys, did you see what she said?

1ST COMIC What did she say?

STRAIGHT Well, she...said...that...I...could...
    MEET HER ROUND THE CORNER, etc.

    (Same business as before. On bump HE hurts his back and limps off.)

2ND COMIC *(wiping his eyes)* Hey, watch it, will you?

1ST COMIC Ladies and gentlemen, you will now be entertained by the Shedhouse Brothers.

    (HE winces again. The triangle sounds. BOTH sing. On "SHE WAS A PEARL," 3RD GIRL enters. Same business as before. SHE drops pocketbook in front of 2ND COMIC, then waits at R. proscenium. SHE shakes every muscle in her body.)

2ND COMIC The lady dropped her pocketbook. Maybe she'll give us a reward.

1ST COMIC Let's get the money first.

(Elaborate business here. THEY look in purse, find no money. THEY dig in with more determination. We hear a small tear. A sheepish exchange of looks between them and a furtive glance at the GIRL, who hasn't heard anything and is not looking at them. 2ND COMIC ad libs, "Damn, her motor's running;" "She must be on relief," etc. Now THEY shrug and rip it deliberately.)

2ND COMIC Oh, oh.

(The purse is in shreds. 1ST COMIC hold it by a thread.)

1ST COMIC *(handing purse to 2ND COMIC)* Here. You give it back to her.

2ND COMIC *(taking it sheepishly)* That's going to be noticeable as hell. *(HE approaches her with the purse. SHE is still shaking.)* I hate to disturb her. So much of her is having a good time. *(HE puts his hand on her shoulder. Her shaking causes him to shake, too. Finally, HE stops her.)* Pardon me, miss, you dropped your pocketbook.

3RD GIIRL *(not taking notice of the damage)* Thank you. And I can see that all my money is still there.

(Both COMICS look startled.)

1ST COMIC It should be. We couldn't find it.

3RD GIIRL Just...for...that...you... can...
MEET ME ROUND THE CORNER, etc.

(SHE bumps and exits. Spotlight from her pelvis knocks off 2ND COMIC's hat. The hat flies into 1ST COMIC's hands.)

1ST COMIC I got it right here in the hat. *(HE hands the hat to 2ND COMIC who looks into it thoughtfully.)*

2ND COMIC If that don't grow hair, nothing will. *(HE puts hat on.)* Hey, _____, did you see what she said? She...said...that...I... could...
MEET HER ROUND THE CORNER, etc.

(As before, but 2ND COMIC is more enthusiastic than the other men. 1ST COMIC gets ready to catch spotlight, ad libbing remarks like, "Put her here, boy;" "Atta, boy." When 2ND COMIC gets to third repetition, and we expect him to end with a bump, HE refuses to stop and does a fourth "MEET ME ROUND THE CORNER." The DRUMMER picks up the tempo. 1ST COMIC runs his partner off.)

1ST COMIC *(alone)* You will now be entertained by Mr. Shedhouse himself.

...Mr. Shedhouse himself.

I WANT A GIRL
JUST LIKE THE GIRL
THAT MARRIED DEAR OLD DAD.
SHE WAS A PEARL...
(No GIRL appears. 1ST COMIC sneaks a peek at the wings and starts over.)

Pearl, Joan, Lisa? Must have run out of girls.
I WANT A GIRL
JUST LIKE THE GIRL...
(Sees no GIRL)

Looks like I've got to change my tune. *(HE sings again.)*
MONEY, MONEY,
MONEY GETS THE HONEY ALL THE TIME.
(4TH GIRL enters hastily, adjusting her dress as if nervous about missing cue. SHE throws her pocketbook down like the other three GIRLS. 1ST COMIC picks it up. HE is impatient with her.)

Pardon me, miss, you dropped your pocketbook, and me bein' a Southern-fried chicken, I'm goin' to return it to you. *(HE hands it to her.)*

4TH GIRL Thank you, and I see all my money is still there. And just for that...you...can...*(DRUMMER starts.)*
MEET ME ROUND THE CORNER
IN A HALF...

1ST COMIC Wait a minute, honey. *(DRUMMER and GIRL stop. 1ST COMIC beckons to her. SHE joins him C.)* There were three girls out here. They all said:
MEET ME ROUND THE CORNER
IN A HALF AN HOUR...
(Does a little grind)

My three friends were weak. They went round the corner. *(very tough)* But I don't go round no corners. Anything you want to do or say to me, you can do right here.

4TH GIRL *(rubs his stomach)* Oh, please.

1ST COMIC *(wilting a bit)* No, I don't go round no corners.

4TH GIRL Oh, won't you please come round the corner?

1ST COMIC *(weak with excitement)* Lady...

4TH GIRL Yes?

1ST COMIC Won't you please make bigger circles? *(SHE does so, making wrinkles in his shirt front)* Look, you've taken the starch out of my dickey.

4TH GIRL *(counting his buttons from collar to waist)* Eeny, meeny, miney, moe...

1ST COMIC *(stopping her hands)* That's as far as you can go.

4TH GIRL *(rubbing again)* Now, will you come around the corner?

1ST COMIC *(very sadly)* Oh, honey, it's too late now.

BLACKOUT

...make bigger circles?

Burlesque performers were constantly at war with self-appointed reformers and censors. In Boston, a one-armed critic named Kelly used to sneak into the Old Howard in order to gather evidence of obscenity that could be used to shut the theatre down. The management installed a signal light in the foots, operated by a switch from the box office. When the cashier saw Kelly approach, he pulled the switch. Dances and skits became suddenly demure, disappointing the audience but frustrating the censor.

In 1942, Mayor Laguardia, under pressure from religious groups, banned Burlesque in New York, thus forcing afficianados to make weekly pilgrimages to Union City and Newark.

Needless to say, the antipathy that reformers felt for Burlesque entertainers was reciprocated. And the comics lost no opportunity to poke fun at hypocritical moralists.

As a result, one of the most popular flirtation scenes of the thirties was the reform scene. In its original version, it took place in front of a night club that was being picketed by the Society for the Suppression of Vice. As scarlet women entered the night club, the pickets lost their moral fervor and followed them.

My variation on this scene (prepared with David Campbell for *Honky Tonk Nights*) is bolder than Burlesquers would have dared to be in 1930. The central joke (the dressmaker sequence) is borrowed from the repertoire of the greatest of all black Burlesque comics, Dewey "Pigmeat" Markham. Markham was for many years the top banana at the Apollo Theatre on 125th St. (formerly Hurtig and Seaman's Music Hall). The Apollo converted from white Burlesque to black Vaudeville and Burlesque in 1935.

BRINGING IN THE SHEAVES
("Reform")

As the GIRLS exit from a number with some "Girlie Dialogue," 1ST COMIC, 2ND COMIC and 3RD COMIC enter from the back of the house. 1ST has a bass drum, 2ND a tuba and 3RD has cymbals. THEY are singing. The scene takes place downstage of the street drop.

ALL. REPENT! REPENT!
    BEFORE YOU'RE OLD AND BENT.
    IF YOU ARE STEEPED IN LUST AND SIN,
    IF ALL YOU EVER GIVE IS IN,
    WE'LL COMFORT YOU THROUGH THICK AND GIN.
    REPENT! REPENT!

(TWO GIRLS from the previous number, now in bathrobes, peek around the corner of the proscenium.)

1ST GIRL Here come those Bible busters again.

2ND GIRL They've been down here four times this week.

BISHOP BENDOVER (1ST COMIC) I prayed for you last night, sister.

1ST GIRL Well, you could have had me, Bishop. I was here all night.

DEACON TOSSPOT (2ND COMIC) She's a fallen woman, brother. Turn a deaf ear.

2ND GIRL Be careful with that mouth of yours, Deacon. The last man who insulted me got what was coming to him.

DEACON Oh? And what did he call you?

2ND GIRL A two-bit floozie.

TOSSPOT So?

2ND GIRL So I hit him over the head with a bagful of quarters.

(The GIRLS exit laughing.)

15

PREACHER DUNKWELL (3RD COMIC) That brazen, shameful, good-looking hussy!

BENDOVER It's time she met her maker.

TOSSPOT Amen.

DUNKWELL We sure came to the right place.

TOSSPOT You said it, Preacher Dunkwell. This here's the devil's doorstep.

BENDOVER Amen! If sin was snowflakes, this place would be a blizzard.

TOSSPOT We'd better do some serious soul-saving tonight.

BENDOVER Right you are, Deacon Tosspot. If I don't collect some sinners pretty soon, they're going to close my mission down and open up a butcher shop.

TOSSPOT Here comes our first customer.

(Enter 1ST SINNER L. in a short dress, very sexy. SHE stops by L. proscenium and counts a big wad of bills which SHE stuffs in her blouse.)

DUNKWELL I'll handle her.

TOSSPOT I saw her first. *(approaching the GIRL)* How do you do, miss? I'm Deacon Tosspot from the Land of Hope and Glory Mission.

1ST SINNER You some kind of priest, Deacon?

TOSSPOT No, I'm a lay preacher. Do you live around here?

1ST SINNER Yes, indeed.

TOSSPOT What do you do?

1ST SINNER I'm a dressmaker.

TOSSPOT Can you make a living that way?

1ST SINNER Sure can, Deacon.

TOSSPOT Well, that's a nice respectable way to earn your daily bread.

1ST SINNER Yes. *(SHE hands him a card from her purse.)* Why don't you come to my shop sometime? I'd like to show you my frocks.

TOSSPOT I don't mind if I do. Will you have anything on at eight o'clock?

1ST SINNER Not a thing.

TOSSPOT I'll be up at seven forty-five.

1ST SINNER Toodle-oo! *(SHE exits.)*

BENDOVER Why did you let her go?

TOSSPOT She has a divine right.

BENDOVER Her left isn't bad either. She sure could decorate a prayer meeting.

> *(Enter 2ND SINNER, sexier than the 1ST. Same business with money at L. proscenium.)*

DUNKWELL This one's mine. *(approaching 2ND SINNER, who is shaking and shimmying)* Pardon me, young lady. Do you live around here?

2ND SINNER Yes, sir.

DUNKWELL What do you do?

2ND SINNER I'm a dressmaker.

DUNKWELL Can you make a living that way?

2ND SINNER Sure can, Preacher.

DUNKWELL. Well, I might have guessed. I can tell you are a nice respectable girl.

2ND SINNER Thank you, Preacher. Why don't you come to my shop sometime? I'd like to give you a swatch of my fabric.

DUNKWELL That's a tempting offer, but I can't.

2ND SINNER Why not?

DUNKWELL It's Lent.

2ND SINNER Well, when you get it back, come on over. *(SHE exits, and HE rejoins the OTHERS.)*

DUNKWELL That's a well-reared woman, Bishop.

BENDOVER She's pretty good in front, too. But that doesn't get us anywhere. *(3RD SINNER [SOUBRETTE] enters L.; same business as before.)* Watch me, brothers; I'll show you how it's done. *(HE crosses to 3RD SINNER.)* Good evening, young lady. Do you live around here?

3RD SINNER. Yes, Bishop.

BENDOVER What do you do?

3RD SINNER. I'm a streetwalker.

BENDOVER A streetwalker?

3RD SINNER. Yes, and a darn good one, too.

BENDOVER Can you make a living that way?

3RD SINNER. I could if it wasn't for all those damned dressmakers.

BENDOVER Well, my little fallen angel, you're more to be petted than censured. I'd be very pleased to wrestle for your soul.

DUNKWELL. So would I.

TOSSPOT You could shake a tambourine at my mission any day.

3RD SINNER. Well, business has fallen off lately. Is there any money in the soul-saving line?

DUNKWELL Yes, indeed.

3RD SINNER How's the passing of the plate at your cathedral?

DUNKWELL Fair to middlin', sister, fair to middlin'. I got a new system for dividing up the proceeds.

3RD SINNER Tell me about it, brother. Tell me.

DUNKWELL Well, every Sunday, I draw a circle on the ground. I take the money from the collection plate and throw it up into the air. Anything that falls inside the circle, I give to the Good Lord; anything that falls outside the circle, I keep for myself.

TOSSPOT Hallelujah! At the Land of Hope and Glory, I do almost the same thing. Only I draw a line on the ground. I throw the money from the collection plate up into the air. Anything that falls to the right of the line, I give to the Good Lord. Anything that falls to the left, I keep for myself.

BENDOVER Learn from me. Learn from me. I, too, throw the money from the collection plate into the air. What the Good Lord wants, He keeps. What falls to the earth, I keep for myself.

3RD SINNER *(hooking her arm into BENDOVER's)* Hallelujah! Bishop, you're my kind of man.

BLACKOUT

Like the *sogetti* of the *commedia dell'arte*, the scenes of Burlesque were built on an expandable-collapsible principle. All the comics and straight men knew stock jokes which could be used to pad out a sketch. Similarly if economy was required, a scene could be stripped of all elaboration and presented as a "blackout," *i.e.*, a scene of two minutes or less.

Here is a famous flirtation sketch, reduced to a blackout. I prepared it for emergency use in *Sugar Babies*. It seemed important to have utility scenes available in case an extra minute was needed for a costume change or a scenery adjustment.

We never had to play this particular piece, I'm happy to say. It is presented here as a typical Burlesque joke, but of the most unsophisticated kind.

I represent the Stingem Charity Association.

THE BLIND BOOTLEGGERS
("The Coin Scene")

Street scene. 1ST COMIC enters in a hurry. 2ND COMIC stops him.

2ND COMIC Where are you going, _____?

1ST COMIC My mother-in-law ate some cucumbers, and she's not expected to live.

2ND COMIC Are you going for the doctor?

1ST COMIC No, more cucumbers. *(enter GIRL)*

GIRL Hello, boys. I represent the Stingem Charity Association. I'm taking up a collection for the blind bootleggers. Won't you please give me something?

1ST COMIC All I have is a dime.

GIRL When I get a dime, I always put it in my shoe. *(SHE does so. COMICS mug. SHE turns to 2ND COMIC.)* Won't you help, too, kind sir?

1ST COMIC Here's a quarter.

GIRL When I get a quarter, I always put it here. *(SHE puts it in a little purse attached to her leg just below the knee.)*

1ST COMIC I'm feeling a little more generous. Here's fifty cents.

GIRL A half a dollar always goes here. *(SHE puts it in purse above knee.)*

2ND COMIC The blind bootleggers is a good cause. I'm not broke yet. Here's a dollar bill. *(1ST COMIC gets down on floor to watch.)*

GIRL That's very kind of you. When I get a dollar bill, it always goes right here. *(COMICS watch as SHE raises dress, then puts money instead in the neck of her bodice. SHE exits.)*

1ST COMIC You damn fool.

2ND COMIC What do you mean?

1ST COMIC Why didn't you give her seventy-five cents?

BLACKOUT

20

Just as jokes have a predictable rhythm and structure, so do many Burlesque bits. The next pair of sketches are "double victim" scenes—scenes in which the comic is fooled by a fast-talking straight man, tries to get even by playing the same trick on someone else and loses a second time. Often the premise in these sketches is some kind of sucker bet. But occasionally the scene is presentational with the straight man acting as a vaudeville performer, a sharpshooter, for example, or a magician—and the comic as an innocent from the audience.

My favorite sketch of this latter type is "The Egg in the Hat," which creates a universe as absurd as anything dreamed up by Ionesco.

AN EGGCENTRIC MAGICIAN
("The Egg in the Hat")

STRAIGHT enters from R. as the GREAT YOGI, wearing a turban and magician's robe and pushing on a small table of props.

YOGI Good evening, ladies and gentlemen. I am the great Yo-gi. [pronounced Yo-guy] For my first display of magic, I need a man with a derby hoot. [rhymes with foot]

LEADER OF THE ORCHESTRA *(from the pit)* You mean a derby hat.

YOGI That's what it was last year, but this year it's a hoot. *(1ST COMIC enters L. HE is wearing a derby hat.)* And here comes a young man with just the sort of hoot I need. Pardon me, young man, I'm the great Yo-gi.

1ST COMIC *(stopping to the R. of YOGI)* The great who-guy?

YOGI The Great Yo-gi. I can use you.

1ST COMIC *(starting to go)* Oh, no, I've been used before.

YOGI I'm a magician. I make small things big.

1ST COMIC *(stopping)* Maybe I can use you. *(HE comes to R. of table.)*

YOGI Would you like to see my big trick?

1ST COMIC I'll take a peek at it.

YOGI I keep my trick in a box.

1ST COMIC The son-of-a-gun ships it by freight.

> *(YOGI opens the box and takes from it a cylinder, which looks suspiciously like a tomato can painted black. HE holds the cylinder in his left hand and picks up a wand from the table with his right.)*

YOGI I have here a magic su-*land*-er.

1ST COMIC Just an old tomato can.

YOGI I tap it with my magic wand. *(taps it)* Nothing here. *(turns it* *around and taps it again)* Nothing there. *(puts wand through cylinder)* Notice the wand passes right through the su-land-er.

1ST COMIC *(to AUDIENCE)* Isn't that marvelous?

YOGI Now, I need your derby hoot.

1ST COMIC That's a hat.

YOGI It's a hoot.

1ST COMIC Well, it's my best hoot.

YOGI Then put your best hoot forward.

1ST COMIC *(holding out his hat)* What are you going to do?

YOGI I'm going to put my trick in it.

1ST COMIC *(pulling his hat toward him protectively)* Not in my hoot, you're not.

YOGI Don't worry. I've been doing this sort of thing for years. If I put anything in your hoot, I'll say some magic words and take it out. *(HE reaches for the hat, takes it and places it upside down on the table.)*

1ST COMIC You better take it out.

YOGI Trust me, young man. *(HE reaches under the table and produces an egg.)* Now, I have here an ordinary hen's eeg. [rhymes with league]

1ST COMIC That's an egg.

YOGI It's an eeg. This outer part here is called the sha-*heel*.

1ST COMIC And I suppose the yellow part inside is the yo-*kal*.

YOGI It's the *yo*-kel. *(1ST COMIC sulks. YOGI picks up the wand.)* Now, I take my magic wand, and I go tap, tap, tap, tap and lo! Nothing happens.

1ST COMIC No wonder.

YOGI Oh?

1ST COMIC You didn't hit the sha-heel.

YOGI Very observant, young man. Now I go tap, tap, tap again. *(taps shell)* And lo, a crack appears!

1ST COMIC You have the strength of a brute.

YOGI Have you ever seen a more beautiful crack?

1ST COMIC Sure.

YOGI On a hen's eeg?

1ST COMIC No, on a duck's ogg. This guy is screwy.

YOGI (*putting down his wand and beginning to squeeze the egg slowly and with apparent effort*) Now, I squeeze, squeeze, squeeze, and look what comes through the crack.

1ST COMIC The yo-kel?

YOGI That's right. I squeeze, squeeze, squeeze, squeeze again, and lo and behold, you now have an eeg in your hoot.

1ST COMIC (*looking into hat*) It better not stay there.

YOGI It won't, young man. It won't. (*reaches into the container and takes out a handful of sawdust*) Now, in my right hand, I have some of my famous magic pow-*dair*.

1ST COMIC That's plain old saw-*doost*.

YOGI (*as HE sprinkles the sawdust into hat*) I go fuzzy wuzzy, wuzzy, wuzzy...(*then suddenly, to an imaginary man*) Get away from me, boy. You bother me. (*HE shakes his leg as if the imaginary man is clutching his trousers.*)

1ST COMIC (*nervously*) You see someone there?

YOGI Yes, he's a little fellow. He's been following me around all day.

1ST COMIC (*edging away from YOGI*) He has?

YOGI Yes, and he's not alone.

1ST COMIC Who's with him?

YOGI A flock of flying oysters. (*ducking*) Watch out! They're swooping down on us! (*appropriate noise from the PERCUSSIONIST*)

1ST COMIC You see flying oysters?

YOGI Yes. (*taking pistol from his pocket*) But I'm ready for them. (*shoots twice*) That scares them away. Now, where was I?

1ST COMIC Getting the eeg out of my hoot.

YOGI Oh, yes. I sprinkle in a little more of the pow-dair. I go fuzzy wuzzy, wuzzy, wuzzy, and then I say the magic words: (*HE chants the following nonsense verse while executing a silly dance in place. While dancing HE uses the cylinder to stir up the mixture in the hat.*)
Abra-cadabra, buzz, buzz bil-i-ous,
Buzz, buzz, bob bob-a-loo.
Abra-cadabra, buzz, buzz bil-i-ous
Buzz, buzz, bob bob-a-loo.
And now, the eeg is out of the hoot. (*HE takes the cylinder out of the hat. 1ST COMIC sulks.*)

1ST COMIC Oh, no, it ain't.

YOGI *(looking into the hat)* Oh, my goodness, something went wrong. *(HE looks quickly at the bottom of the can.)*

1ST COMIC You might say that.

YOGI Maybe I didn't use enough pow-dair. *(stirs in more)* Fuzzy wuzzy, wuzzy. Now, let's try again.
Abra-cadabra, buzz, buzz bil-i-ous,
Buzz, buzz, bob bob-a-loo.

1ST COMIC Get the eeg out of my hoot, hot damn you!

YOGI *(to AUDIENCE)* Ladies and gentlemen, I must apologize. I've been performing this trick for more than twenty years, and nothing like this has ever happened to me before. I have forgotten the magic words that would allow me to bring this remarkable display of magic to its astounding conclusion. *(to 1ST COMIC)* And you, sir, have an eeg in your hoot. *(HE exits.)*

1ST COMIC That son-of-a-gun. *(HE puts the hat on the table just as 2ND COMIC enters wearing a derby hat. A dream of revenge possesses him. To AUDIENCE)* This is going to be a damn shame. *(to 2ND COMIC)* Hey, pal, give me your hoot.

2ND COMIC You mean my hat?

1ST COMIC It's a hoot. Don't argue. Just give it to me.

2ND COMIC Why?

1ST COMIC I'm going to ruin the damn thing!

2ND COMIC *(protecting the hat)* Oh, no, you don't.

1ST COMIC Don't worry. I'm a magician. I make small things big. And if you stand right there, I'll show you my big trick.

2ND COMIC You have a big trick?

1ST COMIC Yes, and I'm going to put it right in your hoot.

2ND COMIC This I've got to see.

1ST COMIC Hold your hoot upside down. *(2ND COMIC does so. 1ST COMIC picks up the cylinder.)* Now, I bet you think this is an old toma-to can.

2ND COMIC That's right.

1ST COMIC Well, it ain't. It's a magic su-land-er. *(taps cylinder with wand)* Nothing here. *(turns the can around and taps again)* Nothing there. *(taps 2ND COMIC's head)* Nothing there either. If there was, you wouldn't be out here. *(takes an egg from under the table)* Now, I have here an ordinary hen's eeg.

2ND COMIC That's an oog.

1ST COMIC I thought it was an ogg. The yellow part is called the yo-kel, and this white part is the sha-heel. This is the little sha-heel. The big sha-heel just left. Now I go tap, tap, tap, and nothing happens. You know why? I didn't hit the sha-heel. I go tap, tap, tap again, and lo, a crack appears! You've seen cracks before?

2ND COMIC Many times.

1ST COMIC Now I go squeeze, squeeze, squeeze, and out comes the yo-kel. I go squeeze, squeeze, squeeze again, and the yo-kel drops into the hoot.

(The yolk falls slowly into the hat.)

2ND COMIC *(sniffing)* That's a mighty ripe yo-kel.

1ST COMIC And a mighty nice hoot. Now, I take a little of my magic sawdoost...*(sprinkling sawdust into the hat)*...and I go fuzzy wuzzy, wuzzy, wuzzy...*(to imaginary man)* Get away from me, boy. You bother me.

2ND COMIC Who are you talking to?

1ST COMIC That's Fred. He's a midget, and he ain't alone.

2ND COMIC He ain't. Who's he with?

1ST COMIC A cluster of creeping clams. But don't worry. I'm ready for them. *(takes a springy club from his pocket and beats the floor with it)* That's better. Where was I?

2ND COMIC Stirring up the saw-doost.

1ST COMIC Well, I'll just stir it up some more.

2ND COMIC That's a real mess.

1ST COMIC You're damned right it is! Then I say:
Abra-cadabra, buzz, buzz bil-i-ous,
Buzz, buzz, bob bob-a-loo. *(imitates YOGI's business from before, but in a much faster tempo)*
Abra-cadabra, buzz, buzz bil-i-ous,
Buzz, buzz, bob bob-a-loo.
And now the eeg is out of the hoot!

2ND COMIC *(showing an empty hat to the AUDIENCE)* Damned if it ain't. *(2ND COMIC slaps 1ST COMIC on the back and exits.)*

BLACKOUT

26

The scene that follows was devised by Jean Bedini in the early 1920's. Bedini was considered the best straight man of his era, and he was a much sought after partner for the star comics. In addition, he wrote and edited sketches for other performers.

"You're Not Here" is a classic double victim scene. I adapted it for a Burlesque review featuring Rip Taylor. The original ending seemed a little weak, so I borrowed a joke from "Madame Mousaka," a mind-reading sketch.

The part played by the soubrette can be played by the second comic.

If you're some place else, you're not here.

NOT PRESENT AT PRESENT
("You're Not Here")

COMIC enters swiftly in one. HE is met by the STRAIGHT MAN.

STRAIGHT Hey, _____, where are you going?

COMIC Don't stop me, _____. A man told me to go to Hell at eight o'clock, and I'm a half hour late.

STRAIGHT You sound as if you're having a bad day.

COMIC A bad day! I've got a wife, a girlfriend and a note at the bank, and they're all past due. Besides, I tapped out at the track.

STRAIGHT That's too bad.

COMIC I didn't mind when my horse was late from the post, but when he stopped at the grandstand and asked, "Which way did they go?"

STRAIGHT Well, since you're a gambling fool, I'll give you a chance to get even. I'll bet you a hundred dollars that you're not here.

COMIC I'm not where?

STRAIGHT Not here.

COMIC *(aside)* Should I take advantage of a crazy man? Of course, I should. *(HE puts a hundred dollars on the floor; STRAIGHT does the same.)*

STRAIGHT All right. Now, you're not in Chicago?

COMIC No, I'm not in Chicago.

STRAIGHT And you're not in New York?

COMIC No, I'm not in New York.

STRAIGHT Well, if you're not in Chicago, and you're not in New York, you must be some place else.

COMIC Right.

STRAIGHT If you're some place else, you're not here. *(grabs money and exits)*

COMIC That son of a biscuit. How did he do that? *(enter SOUBRETTE)* Oh, oh. Here comes a pigeon. I'll get my money back. Hello, _____. I hear that you're a betting woman.

SOUBRETTE I've been known to have a flutter. *(shimmies)*

COMIC We're talking about gambling now. I'll bet you two hundred dollars that you're not here.

SOUBRETTE That's a sucker bet.

COMIC *(aside, gleefully to the AUDIENCE)* You bet it is. *(SHE raises skirt and gets money from a garter above her knee.)*

SOUBRETTE I'll see that two hundred...*(raises skirt. SHE has another garter higher up on her leg. Takes money from second garter.)*...and raise you a hundred.

> *(SHE bends down to place money on the floor. COMIC bends with her, looks down her bodice.)*

COMIC *(aside)* The poor girl has T.B., two beauts. *(HE puts his money on pile.)*

SOUBRETTE All right. Pinch me, _____. That will prove I'm here.

COMIC That's a tempting offer, but I've got to ask you some questions first.

SOUBRETTE Go ahead.

COMIC You're not in Chicago, are you?

SOUBRETTE No, I'm not in Chicago.

COMIC And you're not in New York?

SOUBRETTE No, I'm not in New York.

COMIC If you're not in Chicago, and you're not in New York, you must be some place else.

SOUBRETTE Yes.

COMIC If you're some place else, you're not here. *(SOUBRETTE picks up money and starts to exit.)*

SOUBRETTE Right. Thanks for the bet, _____.

COMIC Wait. That's my money.

SOUBRETTE No, it's not. You said I'm not in New York, and I'm not in Chicago.

COMIC Right.

SOUBRETTE If I'm not in New York, and I'm not in Chicago, I must be some place else.

COMIC Right.

SOUBRETTE If I'm some place else, I'm not here.

COMIC Right.

SOUBRETTE If I'm not here, how did I take your money?

COMIC *(as SHE starts to exit)* Right. No, come back. Double or nothing. Give me a chance to get even.

SOUBRETTE Don't you ever learn?

COMIC I'm a mind reader. I'll bet you four hundred dollars I can answer any question you ask me.

SOUBRETTE Any question?

COMIC That's right.

SOUBRETTE I'll take that bet. *(THEY put money on the floor.)* O.K., you're so smart. Tell me where my father is.

COMIC *(thinking)* Your father is in Jersey City.

SOUBRETTE *(reaching for money)* You lose. My father's been dead for ten years.

COMIC *(taking money from her)* Oh, no. The man your mother married has been dead for ten years, but your father's in Jersey City.

BLACKOUT

The scene I call "Charity Work" is actually a hybrid. It incorporates the best parts of two popular Burlesque bits: "The Ice Cream Scene" and "The Tin Cup." The original "Ice Cream Scene" ends with some distasteful scatological jokes. An angry customer substitutes limburger cheese for a brick of ice cream. The substitution leads the comic to believe that the straight man has become incontinent.

I wanted to preserve the first part of the sketch without relying on the smelly cheese finish. So, I borrowed the last moments of "The Tin Cup" with its unsentimental and completely unexpected ending.

Incidentally, "The Tin Cup" contains a typical Burlesque routine that is worth noting. The comic garbles the speech that the straight man has taught him in a progressively more bizarre way each time he repeats it. Burlesquers called this "doing a Sim Dempsey." "Sim Dempsey" was the name of a minstrel show afterpiece in which the device was first employed.

COMIC discovered standing by small ice cream cart on which the following is painted:

        10
    Ice Cream
        25

HE is ringing a small bell.

COMIC Ice cream. Home made. Ten cents and twenty-five cents. Ice cream.

SOUBRETTE *(entering)* Hello, _____. What flavors have you got?

COMIC Cherry, vanilla, chocolate, banana, strawberry, coconut and *pis*-tachio.

SOUBRETTE Give me vanilla. I'll take six. *(COMIC reaches into cart, begins counting out bricks of ice cream wrapped in tin foil. HE gets to four.)* Oh, I've changed my mind.

COMIC You did?

SOUBRETTE I'll take half a dozen.

COMIC Now, I've got to count them all over. *(HE throws ice cream back into cart, then picks up the bricks again and counts to five.)*

SOUBRETTE One more.

COMIC How many you got?

SOUBRETTE Five. One more.

COMIC That's six?

SOUBRETTE Yes.

COMIC That's half a dozen?

SOUBRETTE Yes.

COMIC I didn't know that. You learn something new every day.

SOUBRETTE How much is it?

COMIC Ten cents each.

SOUBRETTE How much altogether?

COMIC One for ten cents each.

SOUBRETTE But I want to pay for the whole thing.

COMIC Well, you have to figure it out.

SOUBRETTE You figure it out.

COMIC *(scratching numbers on top of his cart with an icepick)* Let's see. Six times one...Say, how do you make a six?

SOUBRETTE It's a nine upside down.

(COMIC goes to the other side of the cart. HE scratches a "9" on cart with icepick. HE returns to his original position, looks at the figure.)

COMIC Oh, yeah. I didn't know that. Six times a half a dozen is four hundred ninety-eight. Four hundred ninety-eight multiplied by one times ten cents each is two million, three hundred sixty-eight thousand...No. That can't be right. I did the addition and subtraction, but I forgot to do the gazinta.

SOUBRETTE What's gazinta?

COMIC That's like seven gazinta two; you can't do it, so you gotta push it in. You give it one good push, it comes out one for ten cents each. You see, it's the same damn thing. I'll give you a break. $1.98.

SOUBRETTE $1.98? When I went to school, six times ten was sixty.

COMIC Well, we won't argue. Thirty-five cents for the whole lot. *(SOUBRETTE looks for money, but can't seem to find it.)* Give me a nickel before it melts.

SOUBRETTE Gee, _____, a funny thing happened this morning.

COMIC What?

SOUBRETTE I went to the store to buy some groceries. I gave the man a ten-dollar bill, and I forgot to get the change.

COMIC That's bad. I suppose you're going to tell me you've got no money to pay for the ice cream?

SOUBRETTE You took the words right out of my mouth.

COMIC I'll take the ice cream right out of your hands. *(does so)*

SOUBRETTE You're nothing but a cheapskate.

COMIC Oh, yeah?

SOUBRETTE Oh, yeah. This is for you. *(snaps fingers)* That's for you. *(snaps fingers)* And that's for your old man. *(flips dress and exits)*

COMIC Dad always gets the best of everything. *(rings bell)* Ice cream. Ten cents and twenty-five cents.

2ND GIRL *(entering)* Hi, _____. What flavors have you got?

COMIC Cherry, vanilla, chocolate, banana, strawberry, cockanut and *pis*-tachio.

2ND GIRL I'll take banana.

COMIC *(handing her large brick)* Here's a nice big one.

2ND GIRL I changed my mind. I'll take chocolate instead.

COMIC *(showing her brick)* I only have small ones.

2ND GIRL That's all right.

COMIC *(handing her small brick)* Here's your chocolate.

2ND GIRL *(handing him large brick)* Here's your banana. *(starts to exit)*

COMIC Hey, come back here. *(2ND GIRL stops.)* What is this, a charity institution?

2ND GIRL Why?

COMIC You didn't pay me for that ice cream.

2ND GIRL *(indicating bricks)* I gave you *that* one for *this* one.

COMIC You didn't pay me for that one.

2ND GIRL I didn't take it, did I?

COMIC No, I still got it.

2ND GIRL By the way, _____, how much is that one?

COMIC Twenty-five cents.

2ND GIRL How much is this one?

COMIC Ten cents.

2ND GIRL Then you owe me fifteen cents.

COMIC *(paying her)* Damned if I don't.

2ND GIRL Be careful, _____, you're going to lose customers if you try to cheat them that way. *(exits)*

COMIC It's costing me money to work this job. Ice cream.

(Enter STRAIGHT MAN.)

STRAIGHT Well, if it isn't _____, my old school chum. You remember me?

COMIC Sure, what are you doing these days?

STRAIGHT I'm just back from the Klondike. Struck oil up there. Made my second million.

COMIC Klondike? Where's that?

STRAIGHT Near the North Pole.

COMIC How's the population up there?

STRAIGHT Lots of people. Lots of people.

COMIC Any Jewish people up there?

STRAIGHT No, I don't think so.

COMIC Well, who's that fellow Iceberg?

STRAIGHT Don't be silly. An iceberg is a great big piece of frozen water.

COMIC No wonder he didn't answer my letters.

STRAIGHT Well, that's enough about me. What are you doing?

COMIC Selling ice cream.

STRAIGHT How's business?

COMIC Not so good. I only made forty thousand dollars last week, but then it was raining. I only worked two days.

STRAIGHT No wonder you're not making any money. You're selling your ice cream too cheap. Two for five.

COMIC Two for five. Where do you see "Two for Five?" *(pointing to the "10")* What's this? One for nothing? It's ten cents and twenty-five cents.

STRAIGHT I didn't see the cents.

COMIC Well, that's right. There's no cents here, no cents there, no sense in the whole damn thing.

STRAIGHT Well, I gotta go, _____. My wife's throwing a party tonight.

COMIC That's nice. My wife threw a party last night.

STRAIGHT She did?

COMIC Yeah, down the stairs. I was the party. *(sudden thought)* Say, if your wife's entertaining, you're going to need some ice cream. How about giving an old friend a break? Get it from me.

STRAIGHT O.K., I will, _____.

COMIC How much will you need?

STRAIGHT Let's see. There'll be two hundred in the gold room, three hundred in the blue room...

COMIC How many in the men's room?

STRAIGHT Give me two chocolate and one vanilla.

COMIC Give you? I don't give them away. I sell them.

STRAIGHT I tell you what. I'll trade you for it.

COMIC Trade me what?

STRAIGHT You give me all the ice cream in the cart, and I'll give you this tin cup. *(produces it)*

COMIC My mother didn't raise a half-wit.

STRAIGHT No. This cup is very valuable. It's a one-of-a-kind cup. I made my first million with it.

COMIC Really? How?

STRAIGHT By begging. I'll toss in the whole routine free of charge.

COMIC You made a million with it?

STRAIGHT Absolutely!

COMIC Let's hear it.

STRAIGHT Hold the cup out like this. And every time someone passes by, you say, "I'm taking up a collection for a poor family named Smith. The father's in jail, and the mother's at home with twelve starving kids. Won't you please give me some money?"

COMIC And that works?

STRAIGHT You'll be rolling in it.

COMIC All right. Here's your ice cream.

STRAIGHT Here's your one-of-a-kind cup. *(HE takes another cup from his pocket and exits with cart. COMIC practices spiel under his breath, as 3RD GIRL comes on trying to do a cartwheel.)*

COMIC What's the matter, young lady?

3RD GIRL I'm going to stand on my head or bust.

COMIC You'll get a better balance on your head.

3RD GIRL What are you doing with that cup?

COMIC I'm mistaking an injection for a poor woman named Smith. She's in jail, and her father's at home with twelve starving children. Won't you please give me something?

> *(3RD GIRL drops coin in cup on string and pulls it out.)*

3RD GIRL *(exiting)* Oh my yes. Oh my yes.

COMIC I see it, but that doesn't put money in my pocket.

> *(Enter 4TH GIRL doing crossword puzzle.)*

4TH GIRL Say, mister. What's a four-letter word ending in I - T that's found at the bottom of a bird cage?

COMIC Grit.

4TH GIRL Do you have an eraser?

COMIC I'm making up an inspection for a poor Smith. The mother needs bail, and the father's been busy starving twelve children.

> *(During his spiel COMIC looks away, and 4TH GIRL fixes her makeup using the cup as a mirror.)*

4TH GIRL I never carry cash.

COMIC I'll take a check.

4TH GIRL I left my checkbook home. *(SHE exits.)*

COMIC I want my ice cream back.

> *(Enter 5TH GIRL with big roll of bills, which SHE slips in her bodice.)*

5TH GIRL I've been hoarding.

COMIC What street?

5TH GIRL No. I've been saving my money, and I'm on my way to the bank to put $500 in my safety deposit box.

COMIC I'm faking up an infection for a poor smith. The father's in the mother, and they're both in jail with twelve starving kids.

5TH GIRL Your tale has touched my heart. I was taking this money to the bank to put it in my safety deposit box, but, instead, I'm going to give it to you. *(SHE does so, exits into wings. COMIC shoots her. SHE screams.)*

COMIC She was too damned good to live.

BLACKOUT

A lying contest is a familiar premise for a comic sketch. In fact, John Heywood, the privileged wit at the court of Henry VIII, made it the basis of his famous farcical interlude *The Four PP*.

Now I don't suppose that any Burlesque comics were devoted readers of Heywood, and we can't trace the origin of "The Liars" back to Tudor England. But it is worth noting that over the years the same jokes stay funny.

Burlesque, you see, was never topical. Unlike the barbs of stand-up comedians, the gags of the Columbia Wheel comics were not dependent on the latest fad or the current occupant of the White House. Great low comedy from Heywood to W. C. Fields deals with those desires and compulsions which never change: greed, sex, self-deception and the deceptions of others.

THE LIARS

Enter STRAIGHT and TWO COMICS in one.

STRAIGHT Well, boys, the race track is closed, and Nervous Nelly has gone to Boston for the holidays.

2ND COMIC Yep. Things are slow.

1ST COMIC Why don't we go fishing?

2ND COMIC What do you know about fishing?

1ST COMIC My Uncle George was a great fisherman. He didn't use a hook either.

STRAIGHT What did he use?

1ST COMIC He went down to the river and threw a handful of tobacco into the water. Naturally, all the fish helped themselves to a free chew.

STRAIGHT Naturally.

1ST COMIC And when they did, my father hit them on the head. Caught a lot of codfish balls that way.

2ND COMIC That's the worst fish story I ever heard. You're a terrible liar.

1ST COMIC I'm a better liar than you are.

2ND COMIC Nobody's a better liar than I am.

STRAIGHT Twenty dollars says I'm better than either of you.

2ND COMIC It's a bet.

1ST COMIC Let's make it fifty to keep the pikers out.

(THEY put the money on the floor. 2ND COMIC steps on it.)

STRAIGHT What's that for?

2ND COMIC To prevent shrinkage. *(to STRAIGHT)* You start.

39

STRAIGHT Well, I'm at a disadvantage, boys. I never told a lie before in my life.

1ST COMIC Give him the money.

2ND COMIC No, come back here; make him work for it.

STRAIGHT Gentlemen, my father had a farm.

1ST COMIC Your father had a farm?

STRAIGHT Yes, my father had a farm.

1ST COMIC Was it a big farm?

STRAIGHT No, just a little farm.

1ST COMIC An itsy-bitsy farm?

STRAIGHT Yes, it stretched from New York to Chicago.

1ST COMIC Give him the money.

2ND COMIC No. Make him work for it.

STRAIGHT On that farm, he built a race track.

1ST COMIC It stretched from New York to Chicago?

STRAIGHT That's right. Just a small race track.

1ST COMIC Give him the money.

2ND COMIC No. Make him work for it.

STRAIGHT Well, a race track needs a grandstand.

1ST COMIC That goes without saying.

STRAIGHT So my father built one.

1ST COMIC Was it a big grandstand?

STRAIGHT No, just a small grandstand.

1ST COMIC Small grandstand?

STRAIGHT Small grandstand.

1ST COMIC On a small race track?

STRAIGHT On a small race track.

1ST COMIC From New York to Chicago?

STRAIGHT From New York to Chicago.

1ST COMIC How big was your father's grandstand?

STRAIGHT Not very big. It only stretched a thousand miles.

1ST COMIC Give him the money.

2ND COMIC No, make him work for it.

STRAIGHT And then, gentlemen, I went to college.

1ST COMIC Oh, you went to college?

STRAIGHT Yes, I spent seven years in college, and would you believe it...

1ST COMIC I don't believe a damn thing you say.

STRAIGHT My father started a race.

1ST COMIC Was it a big race?

STRAIGHT No, a small race.

1ST COMIC A small race?

STRAIGHT Yes.

1ST COMIC On a small track?

STRAIGHT On a small track.

1ST COMIC From New York to Chicago?

STRAIGHT From New York to Chicago.

1ST COMIC Did he start many horses?

STRAIGHT No, just a few.

1ST COMIC How many did he start?

STRAIGHT About twenty thousand.

1ST COMIC Are you going to give him that money?

2ND COMIC No, make him work for it.

STRAIGHT Gentlemen, my father started that race when I went to college, and when I returned after seven years...

1ST COMIC Yes?

STRAIGHT The last horse was just coming in. *(HE reaches for money. 2ND COMIC stamps his foot on it.)*

2ND COMIC My father had a farm.

1ST COMIC Your father had a farm?

2ND COMIC Yes, my father had a farm.

1ST COMIC Was it a big farm?

2ND COMIC No, just a little farm.

1ST COMIC Smaller than his father's farm?

2ND COMIC Much smaller.

1ST COMIC How big was it?

2ND COMIC It stretched from Michigan to California.

1ST COMIC Michigan to California...New York to Chicago...All that's left for me is _____* to _____.* Give him the money.

STRAIGHT No. Make him work for it.

2ND COMIC My father grew corn on that farm.

STRAIGHT Was it large corn?

2ND COMIC No, small corn.

STRAIGHT How tall was your father's corn?

2ND COMIC Well, some stalks were so tall...

STRAIGHT Yes?

2ND COMIC ...that they had to cut the tops off...

STRAIGHT Yes?

2ND COMIC ...to let the moon pass by.

1ST COMIC Oh! What did they do with the small stalks?

2ND COMIC Sold them for railroad ties.

1ST COMIC Give this guy the money.

STRAIGHT No, make him work for it.

2ND COMIC And that ain't all my father grew on his farm.

STRAIGHT What else did he grow?

2ND COMIC He grew apples.

STRAIGHT Large apples?

2ND COMIC No, small apples.

STRAIGHT Itsy-bitsy apples?

2ND COMIC Itsy-bitsy apples.

1ST COMIC Were they crab apples?

2ND COMIC No, they were good-natured apples.

STRAIGHT How large were your father's apples?

---

*Two local places.

42

2ND COMIC Well, last summer one of my father's apples...

STRAIGHT Yes?

2ND COMIC ...dropped off the tree and rolled into [LOCAL]...

STRAIGHT Yes?

2ND COMIC ...smashed up against the pole...

STRAIGHT Yes?

2ND COMIC ...and the people from [LOCAL] got drunk on hard cider for six months.

1ST COMIC On one apple?

2ND COMIC On one apple.

1ST COMIC Give him the money.

STRAIGHT No, make him work for it.

2ND COMIC And that ain't all my father grew on his farm.

STRAIGHT What else did your father grow?

2ND COMIC My father grew raspberries.

1ST COMIC Were they wild raspberries?

2ND COMIC No, we had them under control.

1ST COMIC How large were your father's raspberries?

2ND COMIC Well, it took twenty horses two years to pull one razz off one of my father's raspberries. *(2ND COMIC reaches for the money. 1ST COMIC stamps his foot on it.)*

1ST COMIC My father...

STRAIGHT Oh, you've got a father, too?

1ST COMIC Of course, I've got a father.

2ND COMIC I thought your mother won you in a crap game.

1ST COMIC My father was not a farmer.

STRAIGHT Your father was not a farmer?

1ST COMIC He was a boilermaker.

STRAIGHT What kind of boilers did he make?

1ST COMIC All kinds of boilers.

STRAIGHT Were they big boilers?

1ST COMIC Just small boilers.

STRAIGHT Well, how big were these small boilers?

1ST COMIC One of them was three hundred miles high and six hundred miles long.

STRAIGHT Now tell me, why did your father make a boiler three hundred miles high and six hundred miles long?

1ST COMIC To cook his father's raspberry. *(Thumbs nose; takes money)*

BLACKOUT

The roster of Burlesque graduates who became stars in other branches of entertainment is impressive. It includes Leon Errol, Bert Lahr, Fanny Brice, Sophie Tucker, W. C. Fields, Red Skelton, Phil Silvers, Jackie Gleason, Joe E. Brown, Smith and Dale, Blossom Seeley, Barbara Stanwyck, Rags Ragland, Bud Abbott and Lou Costello.

In fact Abbott and Costello never left Burlesque. The movies in which they appeared for Universal were constructed like the old variety farces of Charles H. Hoyt: a loose skeletal plot with room for a series of self-contained comic bits. Abbott and Costello inserted into their movies and radio shows every stock Burlesque sketch that was clean enough to be performed in the more pristine context.

"Who's on First" is a case in point. Although the pair copyrighted this scene, they did not invent it. The sketch evolved from an earlier bit called "Who Dyed," which had been around since the old minstrel days and which as "Baseball Who's Who," had been performed by many Mutual era comedians.*

Another of the scenes which they made popular with movie audiences is "One to Ten," more properly called "One to Zero." Here is my version of it, which we rehearsed for *Sugar Babies*, but never used.

---

*For Joey Faye's account of the development of this scene, see his article in *American Popular Entertainment*, edited by Myron Matlaw, Greenwood Press, 1979, pp. 68-9.

ONE TO TEN

In front of blue traveler. STRAIGHT enters R. TWO COMICS enter L.

STRAIGHT Where are you going, boys?

2ND COMIC We're looking for women.

STRAIGHT Are you looking for any women in particular?

1ST COMIC No, we're looking for women who ain't particular.

2ND COMIC You see, my friend won a buck or two on the numbers, and he's looking for a bum to spend it on.

STRAIGHT Well, you're in luck, boys. Ten beautiful women are meeting here in a few minutes, and I'm going to play games with them.

2ND COMIC In front of all these people?

STRAIGHT Yes.

1ST COMIC They'll close the theatre.

STRAIGHT It's not what you think, boys. Those girls are partners of mine in a little game of chance.

2ND COMIC Oh, you're a betting man?

STRAIGHT That's right. I bet on anything.

1ST COMIC Anything at all?

STRAIGHT You name it.

2ND COMIC I'll bet you $50 I can answer any question you ask me.

STRAIGHT O.K. And just to prove that I'm as smart as you are, I'll bet you $10 that I can answer any question you ask me.

2ND COMIC It's a bet.

STRAIGHT All right, what is it that has four legs, blue feathers, flies upside down like an Australian cuckoo and yodels every other Tuesday?

2ND COMIC I give up. Here's your fifty.

STRAIGHT Thanks.

2ND COMIC By the way, what is it?

STRAIGHT Damned if I know. Here's your ten.

2ND COMIC Well, we broke even on that one.

STRAIGHT Now it's time for some heavy betting.

1ST COMIC *(starts to peel off bills)* Good.

STRAIGHT But before we put our money on the line, let's call in reinforcements. All right, men, front and center. Forward march.

> *(ORCHESTRA plays "STARS AND STRIPES" or similar piece. TEN GIRLS march on. EACH is carrying a placard with a number on it from one to zero. This march can be simply a short entrance piece, or a more elaborate military number.)*

STRAIGHT At ease, men.

2ND COMIC Men? There weren't any men like that in my army.

1ST COMIC How things have changed since mother was a pup.

STRAIGHT Now, boys, this little game is called the Kissing Game. Do you follow me?

1ST COMIC I'm way ahead of you.

STRAIGHT You go over and kiss any girl you like.

1ST COMIC This is my kind of game.

STRAIGHT I turn my back and tell you the number of the girl you kissed.

1ST COMIC You can't do it.

STRAIGHT Money talks.

1ST COMIC Well, here's fifty to get the conversation started. *(STRAIGHT turns back as 1ST COMIC goes over and kisses NUMBER SEVEN.)* All right, I kissed one.

STRAIGHT Let me see now. Was it odd or even?

1ST COMIC *(to 2ND COMIC, undertoning)* Was it odd or even?

2ND COMIC Odd.

STRAIGHT Was it between two and four?

BOTH COMICS Naw. You're way off.

STRAIGHT Was it between four and six?

1ST COMIC No, but you're getting hotter.

STRAIGHT Was it between six and eight?

1ST COMIC Yes.

STRAIGHT Seven. *(HE picks up the money and counts it.)*

1ST COMIC Now how did he do that?

2ND COMIC Damned if I know.

1ST COMIC I've got an idea how we can get our money back.

2ND COMIC How?

1ST COMIC We cheat. We let him do the kissing. You guess. I watch, and then I hit you with this shillelagh. *(takes stuffed club from his back pocket)*

2ND COMIC What for?

1ST COMIC If I hit you three times, that means he kissed number three. If he kisses number five, I give you five good socks where you can't miss it.

2ND COMIC That's a great idea.

1ST COMIC Hey, fella. This time we guess, and you do the puckering. And just to make it fair, let's up the stakes a little. Here's $200.

STRAIGHT I'll see that two hundred and raise you fifty cents.

2ND COMIC He's getting out of our league.

1ST COMIC *(to 2ND COMIC)* Don't worry. *(to STRAIGHT)* You're covered. *(While THEY are looking away, STRAIGHT kisses ONE of the GIRLS.)*

STRAIGHT All right, which one did I kiss?

1ST COMIC *(turning around in amazement)* Why, I didn't see you, and I couldn't tell my friend.

STRAIGHT What?

1ST COMIC I mean I've got to convey the idea to him by mental Western Union.

STRAIGHT You mean mental telepathy?

1ST COMIC Telegraph, that's it. Go ahead.

> *(STRAIGHT starts to kiss NUMBER 6, switches to 7, and 1ST COMIC is not certain which of the two STRAIGHT kissed. HE hits 2ND COMIC six times.)*

LEADER OF THE ORCHESTRA *(from the pit)* One more. *(1ST COMIC hits 2ND COMIC one more time.)*

2ND COMIC S-s-seven.

1ST COMIC Seven. We win. *(HE takes money.)*

STRAIGHT That's not fair. He said six.

1ST COMIC No, it just seemed that way. He stutters when he's excited.

STRAIGHT Well, boys, let's do it one more time.

1ST COMIC Sure, we've got a system now. *(THEY put money down. STRAIGHT kisses ZERO.)*

2ND COMIC Pick a hard one. Pick a hard one.

1ST COMIC He picked a hard one all right. *(STRAIGHT laughs and starts to pick up money. 1ST COMIC kicks 2ND COMIC in pratt.)*

2ND COMIC Oh! *(STRAIGHT stands up. 1ST COMIC picks up money.)*

1ST COMIC It's a damn good thing you didn't say ouch!

BLACKOUT

A body scene, in Burlesque terminology, was a sketch requiring a full-stage set, a cast of some size and perhaps special costumes or a Rube Goldberg prop or two. The next ten sketches fit into this category.

The subject matter of the ten reflects the preoccupations of the working-class patrons of these slum music halls. The action is set in the places that were familiar to those patrons—cheap hotels, courtrooms, greasy spoons, urban schoolrooms, doctors' offices, gambling halls.

The comics themselves spent a lot of time in cheap hotels, so, as you might expect, they developed a large number of hotel sketches. "The Four Door Hotel" chronicles the adventures of the principal comic with a hotel guest who turns out to be a voluptuous somnambulist. Equally risqué is "The Hit and Run Hotel" and "The Baseball Player's Honeymoon." My own favorite is "The Hairbrush Hotel," which we doctored up with a new ending and played for seven and a half years in *Sugar Babies*.

I include also some hotel scenes that I adapted and kept in reserve, but never used. "Up to Be Cleaned" is a sketch of the surrealistic "crazy-house" variety. And "Candles" is a brief piece of cheerful obscenity that might or might not amuse a modern audience.

THE BROKEN ARMS HOTEL
("Hairbrush Hotel")

In darkness, a phone rings. Lights up to reveal a shabby hotel lobby. A desk C. with two upright phones on it. CLERK is discovered behind the desk. At R. is a door leading to one of the rooms.

CLERK *(on the phone)* Hello. Is this Room 19? Are you the lady that left a call for ten o'clock? Well, it's six o'clock. You got four more hours to sleep. *(HE hangs up. Second phone rings.)* Broken Arms front desk. What's that? You say you've got a leak in your bathtub? Well, go right ahead. You paid for the room.

> *(COMIC, looking extremely disheveled, enters from S.R. door. He is wearing pants with suspenders over long winter underwear.)*

COMIC What kind of hotel is this?

CLERK What's the matter, sir?

COMIC I can't get any sleep. There's a woman in the room next to mine. And she must be a candy lover.

CLERK A candy lover?

COMIC Well, all night long she keeps hollering, "Oh, Henry! Oh, Henry." Besides, there's a terrible racket in the room upstairs.

CLERK Oh, I forgot to tell you, sir. They're holding an Elks' Ball up there.

COMIC What?

CLERK They're holding an Elks' Ball.

COMIC *(A look of sympathetic pain crosses his face.)* Well, tell them to let go, so we can get some sleep. Hey, listen, I'm checking out. I'll get my car, and I'll be right back.

> *(HE exits as an OLD MAN and YOUNG GIRL enter. THEY are obviously newlyweds. HE is wearing morning clothes, SHE an abbreviated bridal outfit. HE carries a suitcase.)*

OLD MAN Come on, darlin'. *(to CLERK)* I beg your pardon. Can we have a room for the night? I'd like the bridal suite. We just got married.

CLERK Oh, honeymooners. You can have the bridal suite right over there. *(indicating the room just vacated by COMIC)* Did you come a long way?

YOUNG BRIDE Yes, and now I'm ready to go a lot further. *(starts across to S.R. door)* Hurry up, dear, I can hardly wait. I can hardly wait! *(SHE exits into the room R., and OLD MAN starts to follow her off.)*

OLD MAN *(indicating his heart)* Keep pumping, pal.

CLERK *(stopping OLD MAN)* Oh, sir, that's a very energetic young wife you have there. But there's such a difference in your ages. Couldn't a honeymoon like this prove fatal?

OLD MAN Hey, listen, if she dies, she dies! *(HE exits. Enter COMIC L. HE runs toward S.R. door.)*

COMIC *(yelling to someone offstage)* Keep the motor running. I'll be right back. I left something in the room.

CLERK I'm sorry, sir. You can't go in there. I just rented that room to a newly-married couple. I can't disturb them.

COMIC I tell you I left something in that room, and I'm gonna get it. *(HE walks towards door.)* Besides if they just got married, they won't be asleep.

OLD MAN *(off)* Whose beautiful red lips are those, darlin'?

YOUNG BRIDE *(off)* They're yours, daddy.

OLD MAN *(off)* And whose lily-white shoulders are those?

YOUNG BRIDE *(off)* They're yours, daddy.

OLD MAN *(off)* And whose cute little pink tummy is that?

YOUNG BRIDE *(off)* It's yours, daddy.

COMIC *(shouting at the door)* When you get to the hairbrush, that's mine. *(to CLERK)* Hey, listen, they're busy. When you find it, wrap it up and send it to me by slingshot. *(HE starts to exit.)*

CLERK *(stopping him)* Wait a minute, sir. You forgot your bill.

COMIC My bill?

CLERK *(presenting it)* Yes, that will be a hundred and twenty dollars.

COMIC A hundred and twenty dollars for one night? This must be [LOCAL].

CLERK That's $50 for the room and $70 for the food you and your wife ordered.

COMIC My wife didn't order any food.

CLERK It was there if you wanted it.

COMIC *(angrily giving CLERK some money)* Here's $50, and I'm charging you $70 for fooling around with my wife.

CLERK *(indignantly)* I didn't fool around with your wife.

COMIC It was there if you wanted it. *(HE exits S.L.)*

BLACKOUT

FULL SERVICE HOTEL
("Up to Be Cleaned")

An empty room. No furniture except for a ten-foot ladder. Enter STRAIGHT and COMIC.

STRAIGHT Well, sir, this is the best room in the house. That'll be two dollars a night.

COMIC Two dollars for what? There's no furniture here.

STRAIGHT Oh, sure there is. *(points to imaginary bed R.)* Look at that bird's eye maple bed.

COMIC You see a bed?

STRAIGHT Certainly I see it. And it has a marvelous down mattress.

COMIC That mattress is so far down I can't see it.

STRAIGHT Look at that beautiful sunken bath.

COMIC It's sunken all right.

STRAIGHT And the what-not in the corner.

COMIC Oh, there's a what-not in the corner. That must be valuable.

STRAIGHT Yes.

COMIC Is it antook?

STRAIGHT You mean antique?

COMIC That's the word, but I can't say it.

STRAIGHT Say what?

COMIC Antique. What's the stepladder for? So I can get up in the morning?

STRAIGHT No, a couple of song-and-dance men occupied this room last night, and they must have left their steps behind.

COMIC This is the only room you have?

STRAIGHT The only one.

COMIC Well, I'll take it.

STRAIGHT If you need anything during the night, just call for me. *(pats COMIC's bottom and exits)*

COMIC I'll do that. Well, I can see the pillows on this bed are not going to be high enough for me. So I better use my hat to build them up. *(HE lies on floor and puts hat under his head. The hat is suddenly jerked out from under him. It travels up the edge of the tormentor and disappears into the flies.)* Landlord. Landlord. *(STRAIGHT enters.)*

STRAIGHT What's the matter?

COMIC I wanted a softer pillow, so I put my hat under my head.

STRAIGHT Yes?

COMIC Well, it went zoom up in the air, and I haven't seen it since.

STRAIGHT That's a service of this hotel. Your hat went up to be cleaned. It will be down in the morning.

COMIC It went up to be cleaned?

STRAIGHT Yes.

COMIC It will be down in the morning?

STRAIGHT Exactly. Now, go to bed and have a good night's sleep. *(STRAIGHT starts for door.)*

COMIC Hey, wait a minute, landlord. Take that crazy quilt off the bed, will you? You see, my wife slept under a crazy quilt once, and she lost her mind. *(STRAIGHT takes imaginary quilt from COMIC.)*

STRAIGHT Certainly, sir. And if you want anything in the night, just call me.

COMIC I'll do that. *(COMIC is about to lie down. 1ST GIRL enters R.)*

1ST GIRL Oh, boy, I never had it,
　　Oh, boy, I never had it,
　　Oh, boy, I never had it.

(SHE grinds and bumps and wiggles her way across the stage.)

COMIC Landlord! Landlord! *(STRAIGHT enters.)*

STRAIGHT What's the matter now?

COMIC I never had it.

STRAIGHT What do you mean?

COMIC There was a dame in here, and she was an awful liar, and she said she never had it. *(imitates her bump)*

STRAIGHT Well, that girl never did have it.

COMIC How do you know?

STRAIGHT Well, I know that little girl, and she never had cream in her coffee.

COMIC Oh, is that it? Cream?

STRAIGHT Yes.

COMIC In her coffee?

STRAIGHT Yes, now go to bed. Good night. *(HE exits.)*

COMIC Well, I got to get some sleep, and I've got to have a pillow. *(puts coat under head. It flies up the tormentor into the flies.)* Landlord! Landlord! *(STRAIGHT enters.)* Is this a hotel or a loony bin?

STRAIGHT Why?

COMIC I put my coat down under my head and zoom it went up in the air.

STRAIGHT Well, of course. It went up to be cleaned.

COMIC Oh?

STRAIGHT It will be down in the morning.

COMIC It must go up to be cleaned?

STRAIGHT Yes, but it'll be down in the morning.

COMIC Yes. I've noticed that myself.

STRAIGHT Now, go to bed. I want to get some sleep. *(HE exits.)*

COMIC So do I. So do I.

> *(Starts to lie on the floor. 2ND GIRL enters.)*

2ND GIRL Oh, boy, I really want it,
Oh, boy, I really want it,
Oh, boy, I really want it.

> *(SHE bumps, wiggles, grinds across the stage, then exits.)*

COMIC Landlord! Landlord! *(STRAIGHT enters.)* What the hell is this? A parade?

STRAIGHT Why?

COMIC There was a girl in here who said she really wanted it, and I could tell she really did, but she left too soon.

STRAIGHT You couldn't give her any?

COMIC No.

STRAIGHT Of course not. After all, you haven't got any.

COMIC How the hell do you know?

STRAIGHT Because all the stores are closed this time of night, and you can't get any cream for her coffee.

COMIC Oh, is that what she wanted?

STRAIGHT Yes.

COMIC Well, cream is hard to get.

STRAIGHT Yes.

COMIC And evaporated milk is harder.

STRAIGHT Is it?

COMIC Yes, it takes a lot of work to get a cow to sit on one of those little cans.

STRAIGHT Do me a favor, will you? Go to bed. *(HE exits.)*

COMIC Well, I got to have a pillow. I'd better use my vest. *(As HE starts to lie down on the vest, it is yanked from underneath him. It goes up the tormentor into the flies.)* Landlord! Landlord!

STRAIGHT *(entering)* What's the matter?

COMIC My vest is missing.

STRAIGHT Certainly, it's gone up to be cleaned.

COMIC Up to be cleaned?

STRAIGHT Yes, but it'll be down in the morning. Now, don't disturb my rest again. Good night. *(HE exits.)*

COMIC Well, if you'd just direct the traffic somewhere else. This place is busier than the Holland Tunnel on Sunday.

GIRL *(enters)* Oh, boy, I just had it,
    Oh, boy, I just had it,
    Oh, boy, I just had it.
    (Same business as before. SHE exits.)

COMIC Landlord! Landlord!

STRAIGHT *(entering)* Not you again.

COMIC There was a girl in here, and she just had it. In fact, she was bragging about it.

STRAIGHT Well, no wonder she was bragging.

COMIC It ain't much to brag about.

STRAIGHT Well, you'd brag, too.

COMIC Would I?

STRAIGHT If you'd just had cream in your coffee. Now, don't bother me again. Good night! *(HE exits.)*

COMIC What kind of nuthouse is this?

> *(CHARACTER enters. HE is wearing a long nightshirt and has an eyepatch over his right eye. HE fires a gun four times. The startled COMIC hollers and starts up the ladder as CHARACTER exits and STRAIGHT enters.)*

STRAIGHT Where are you going?

COMIC I'm going up to be cleaned. I'll be down in the morning.

BLACKOUT

I'm going up to be cleaned.

POWER FAILURE
("Candles")

[Note: This scene is played in darkness
except for the two candle flames.]

Enter COMIC with lighted candle.

COMIC Hey, bell hopper. What's the matter with this hotel? The lights are out again. *(Crash as HE hits furniture.)* Son of a biscuit! *(GIRL walks into area illuminated by flame.)* Oh, I beg your pardon, miss.

GIRL Can you tell me where the bellboy is?

COMIC I guess he went out with the lights.

GIRL Isn't that too bad? There's no light in my room.

COMIC That's not too bad. I have the only light in the hotel.

GIRL Would you give me a light on my candle?

COMIC Of course, but I can't give you a light for nothing.

GIRL *(after a short pause)* What do you mean?

COMIC I'll give you a light if you'll give me a kiss.

GIRL *(after slightly longer pause)* I hardly know you.

COMIC I'm just as ashamed of that as you are.

GIRL *(after another pause)* What would mother say?

COMIC I don't want to kiss your mother.

GIRL *(sighing)* Well, I must have a light.

COMIC True, you must have a light, and I've got a light, and you've got what it takes to get a light, so why be without a light?

GIRL All right. Give me the light.

COMIC Give me the kiss first. I've peddled lights before.

GIRL Here's your kiss. *(kissing noise)*

COMIC Here's your light. *(Exchange of lights; the two candles separate.)*

GIRL Ah, me.

COMIC Ah, me, too.

GIRL Good night.

(COMIC blows out his light.)

COMIC Goodness gracious.

GIRL What's the matter?

COMIC My light went out.

GIRL Isn't that a shame. *(BOTH back to center.)*

COMIC It certainly is.

GIRL Now I have the only light in the hotel.

COMIC Yes, you're very lucky. Say, would you give me a light on my candle?

GIRL Of course, but I can't give you a light for nothing.

COMIC I didn't expect it for nothing.

GIRL I'll give you a light if you'll give me a kiss.

COMIC If I must, I must. Give me the light first.

GIRL Give me the kiss first.

COMIC I'm not the only one who's peddled lights before. Here's your kiss. *(kissing noise)*

GIRL. Here's your light. *(Exchange of lights; then the TWO separate.)*

COMIC Good night. *(GIRL blows out light.)*

GIRL Oh, dear, my light is out again.

COMIC So I noticed. *(The COMIC and GIRL come C.)*

GIRL There must be a terrible draft in this hotel.

COMIC I suppose you want another light.

GIRL I suppose you want another kiss.

COMIC Two kisses this time.

GIRL You've raised your price.

COMIC The candle's getting shorter.

GIRL Well, if I must, I must. *(kissing noise)*

COMIC One more. *(louder kissing noise)* I've been in the wrong business all these years.

GIRL Good night.

COMIC Good night. *(The candles separate.)*

GIRL Goodness gracious.

COMIC What's the matter?

GIRL My candle's flickering.

COMIC And mine is running out of wax.

(THEY blow out their candles. Rest of the scene is in darkness.)

GIRL What will we do now?

COMIC We'll think of something.

GIRL Where are you? Oh, there you are. Good heavens, you said your candle was getting shorter.

COMIC That's not my candle.

(ORCHESTRA chord)

BLACKOUT

"Tact" is a joke with a double punch-line. This rhythm makes it perfect for dramatization. I choose it here to represent all the sketches that take place in retail establishments—not only groceries, but also pharmacies, junkyards, candy stores and pawn shops.

I never used this sketch in *Sugar Babies*, but in the workshop of *Honky Tonk Nights*, it was played successfully by Reginald Vel Johnson, Alan Weeks and the late Cleavon Little.

The perceptive reader will notice a few lines from "The Ice Cream Scene" in the first part of this bit. I did not edit them out, because I wanted to demonstrate how transferrable stock jokes can be. As long as you don't use the same cracks twice in the same show, you can borrow from one sketch to reinforce another. Needless to say, if "Ice Cream" and "Tact" were both on the rundown sheet, an excision would be necessary.

TACT
("Grocery Bit")

A grocery store. McSORLEY on the phone.

McSORLEY (STRAIGHT) McSorley's Green Grocer, Patrick Seamus McSorley's speaking...Of course, we deliver...What's that? Your wife is throwing a party tonight? My wife threw a party last night. Down the stairs. I was the party...You want some soda, bread and cheese?...You say there'll be two hundred in the gold room...three hundred in the blue room...How many in the men's room?...You'll need at least a dollar's worth. I'll go back and fill the order myself...Goodbye. *(to COMIC)* O'Hara.

COMIC Yes, sir.

McSORLEY I'll be back in a minute. While I'm gone, straighten up the store. *(exits)*

COMIC I didn't know it was tilted.

(Under his breath, HE starts singing, "REMEMBER, BOY, YOU'RE IRISH." GIRL enters.)

GIRL Say, mister, how much are the grapefruits?

COMIC Thy're ten cents each.

GIRL And how much are the oranges?

COMIC Five cents.

GIRL I'll take a grapefruit.

COMIC *(handing her one)* Here you are.

GIRL *(starts out, then stops)* On second thought, I'll take an orange.

COMIC *(handing her one)* Here's your orange.

GIRL Here's your grapefruit. *(starts to go)*

COMIC Wait a minute, little girl. What do you think this is, a charity institution? You didn't pay for that orange.

GIRL I gave you the grapefruit for the orange.

COMIC *(perplexed)* But you didn't pay for the grapefruit.

GIRL I didn't take it, did I?

COMIC No, it's still here.

GIRL By the way, how much is the grapefruit?

COMIC Ten cents.

GIRL And how much is the orange?

COMIC Five cents.

GIRL You owe me five cents.

COMIC Damned if I don't. *(gives it to her)*

GIRL *(skipping out)* Watch out, mister, you're going to lose customers that way.

COMIC You know, she may be right. *(enter TOUGH CUSTOMER)* What can I do for you, sir?

TOUGH CUSTOMER I want a half a head of lettuce.

COMIC *(picking up a head)* I'm sorry, sir, we don't sell half heads of lettuce.

TOUGH I want what I want when I want it, and right now I want a half a head of lettuce.

> *(Enter McSORLEY with his big order.)*

COMIC I'll have to ask the manager. *(HE walks over to McSORLEY, not noticing that the TOUGH is right behind him.)* Mr. McSorley?

McSORLEY Yes, son.

COMIC There's a big dumb son of a bitch over there who wants a half a head of lettuce...*(looking up and noticing TOUGH)*...and this gentleman wants the other half.

> *(HE slices the lettuce in half with his produce knife and gives half to the TOUGH.)*

TOUGH *(throwing coin down)* That's more like it. *(exits)*

COMIC I'm sorry, Mr. McSorley.

McSORLEY Say nothing of it, my boy. You handled that situation with great tact. I've got my eye on you. I'm opening a branch store in Detroit, and you might be just the man to manage it for me.

COMIC Detroit? There's nothing in Detroit but prostitutes and hockey players.

McSORLEY My wife's from Detroit.

COMIC What team does she play for?

BLACKOUT

There are two types of restaurant scenes: those in which the comic is the patron while the straight man plays the waiter, and those in which the roles are reversed. The classic sketch of the first type is "Cut Up and Bleeding." Two comics order a meal without the wherewithal to pay for it. They agree to start a fight after the dinner is consumed, pretend that they are going to settle their dispute in the alley, leave the restaurant and run like hell. Needless to say, the strategem backfires.

In "Chez Butch" ("Hold That Chicken"), the straight man and the soubrette are elegant patrons of a shabby cafe, and the comic is an aggressive waiter. In the first national company of *Sugar Babies*, Carol Channing played the Waiter (Waitress). This is one of the few scenes in Burlesque in which you can give a woman the punch line.

CHEZ BUTCH
("Hold That Chicken")

A shabby looking restaurant. WAITER (1ST COMIC) is discovered with back to audience. Enter STRAIGHT MAN, a well-dressed man-about-town and his GIRLFRIEND.

STRAIGHT Darling, this is Chez Butch, the most elegant restaurant in town. It fairly reeks with atmosphere.

GIRL I'm so hungry I could eat a horse.

COMIC *(turning around)* Well, you came to the right place. *(A horse whinnies offstage.)* Two for dinner?

STRAIGHT Yes.

WAITER Do you have a reservation?

STRAIGHT No.

COMIC *(consulting his book)* Well, I'll see if I have a table. Yes. I think I can squeeze you in right over here.

STRAIGHT *(sitting)* Well, precious, the night is yours. Order anything you want.

GIRL Oh, daddy, you know what I want.

COMIC Yes, but you better eat first.

STRAIGHT Didn't I tell you what a wonderful old place this is! Look at these chairs. I bet these chairs go back to Louis the Fourteenth.

WAITER No, they go back to Macy's the Fifteenth.

STRAIGHT Where is Willie, the head-waiter?

WAITER He had a tragic accident.

STRAIGHT What happened?

WAITER He was eating one of the cook's steaks. Somebody hollered, "Whoa," and he choked to death. *(a scream offstage)*

STRAIGHT What's that?

WAITER That's the dentist next door. Business is so bad in this part of town, he's pulling his own teeth.

STRAIGHT Could we have menus?

WAITER We don't have menus here. You name it; we've got it.

STRAIGHT I'll have rack of lamb.

WAITER We haven't got it.

GIRL Filet of sole for me.

WAITER We haven't got it.

STRAIGHT Roast beef?

WAITER We haven't got it.

STRAIGHT I thought you said, "You name it; we've got it."

WAITER You haven't named it yet.

STRAIGHT Well, give us a little help. What's the soup of the day?

WAITER We have chicken soup and pea soup.

Hold that chicken…

GIRL I'll take the chicken soup.

WAITER *(calling to kitchen)* One bowl of chicken!

COOK *(offstage, calling from the kitchen, biting line and speaking rapidly)* One bowl of chicken!

WAITER That's my girlfriend, the cook. She's very fast. She used to work for Swift & Company.

GIRL On second thought, I don't want chicken soup.

WAITER *(erasing pad)* You don't?

68

GIRL I want pea soup instead.

WAITER *(calling offstage)* Hold that chicken and make it pea.

STRAIGHT What goes with soup?

WAITER A nice tongue sandwich?

GIRL I never eat anything that comes out of an animal's mouth.

WAITER How about a couple of eggs?

(Enter the COOK with a strangled-looking chicken.)

COOK *(a slatternly FE-MALE)* I've been holding that chicken for five minutes, and I'm damned if I can make it...

GIRL That's it. I've had it. Such rudeness! We're getting out of here. *(SHE and STRAIGHT rise angrily.)*

WAITER Not so fast. You haven't paid your check.

STRAIGHT What check? We didn't eat anything.

WAITER This restaurant has a minimum charge of forty dollars.

STRAIGHT Forty dollars?

WAITER What do you expect? You're in [LOCAL CITY].

STRAIGHT Well, it's worth it to get out of here. *(HE pays the WAIT-ER, as THEY stalk out angrily.)*

COOK *(reaching for money)* I'll take that. The first cash we've made in a month.

WAITER *(keeping money)* No, you don't. I have a use for this money. This restaurant business stinks. I'm leaving, and I'm leaving alone.

COOK Why, you dirty rat. You said you worshipped the ground I walked on.

WAITER I thought your father owned that piece of property.

COOK Where are you going?

WAITER To Pago-Pago. [pronounced Pango-Pango]

COOK Pago-Pago? Why?

WAITER There's a shortage of men there, and the birthrate is falling. So the government has put out a proclamation. Every time a man makes love to a woman, he gets five dollars.

COOK I'm going with you.

WAITER What for?

COOK I want to see how you're going to live on ten dollars a year.*

BLACKOUT

---

*If, as in the Carol Channing version, the waiter (waitress) is a woman, the cook, of course, must be a man, in which case it is the cook who heads for Pago-Pago.

The origin of many Burlesque sketches is obscure. Some of them were based on minstrel-show afterpieces. Others were adapted from Vaudeville turns.

Burlesquers were jealous of performers on the Keith-Albee time and lost no opportunity to steal their material. Jans and Whalen's famous skit, "Packing the Trunk," was dirtied up by Burlesque comics and played for years as "Dressing and Undressing." Also the popular school acts of Gus Edwards and others, which featured aggressively precocious children doing musical and comic specialties, were satirized in the schoolroom scenes that became popular on the Mutual Wheel.

Schoolroom sketches always featured a tough schoolteacher trying to control a class of brats. Since this situation perfectly suited the energetic style of Mickey Rooney, I prepared two of them ("Prose or Poetry" and "My Schooldays Are Over")—one for the original *Sugar Babies* and one for a sequel (still unproduced as of this writing).

Now it's time for poetry...

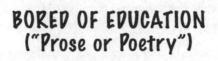

BORED OF EDUCATION
("Prose or Poetry")

ORCHESTRA plays a signature tune. Curtain parts to reveal schoolroom with teacher's desk and four smaller desks for pupils. TEACHER (the PRIMA DONNA) is discovered. SHE is wearing a school-marm dress. SHE has a rolled newspaper in her hands. TWO GIRLS enter. THEY are dressed as third graders and have pigtails. TEACHER rings the bell.

TEACHER Good morning, girls.

GIRLS Good morning, teacher.

TEACHER Where is little _____?

(2ND COMIC enters as child. HE is wearing a middy blouse and knickers.)

2ND COMIC Here I am, teach. Hey, Teach, before class starts, may I ask you a question?

TEACHER Certainly, _____.

2ND COMIC Can an eleven-year old girl have a baby?

TEACHER Certainly not.

2ND COMIC *(to 1ST GIRL, as HE sits)* See, honey, I told you we had nothing to worry about.

TEACHER All right, children. Class will come to order. Where is _____?

(1ST COMIC, wearing short pants, a curly wig and a little cap, enters.)

1ST COMIC I'm sorry I'm late, teach. But I didn't have any breakfast. I didn't have any eggs and bacon. I didn't have any scrapple...

TEACHER Well, sit down, _____. We'll get you breakfast right after lunch. You're just in time for your geography lesson. Tell me, _____, where is the Canadian border?

1ST COMIC In bed with my mother. That's why I didn't get any breakfast. *(TEACHER hits him. HE is aggrieved.)*

TEACHER That's enough geography. Now it's time for history. Tell me, Rose, what happened in 1898?

2ND GIRL *(standing)* The battleship Maine was sunk. *(The PUPILS congratulate her. SHE curtsies into her seat.)*

TEACHER Very good, Rosie. Now, _____, tell me what happened in the year 1900?

1ST COMIC *(standing)* The battleship Maine was sunk two years. *(TEACHER hits 1ST COMIC. HE whines softly, sits, then feels 2ND GIRL's leg. 2ND GIRL slaps his hand coquettishly.)*

TEACHER That's certainly enough of history. Now, it's time for our English lesson. *(The PUPILS ad lib, "Good," "I like English," etc.)* _____, use the words "defense," "defeat" and "detail" in a sentence.

2ND COMIC *De dog* jumped over *de fence*, and *de feet* went over before *de tail*.

1ST COMIC De-pressing.

> *(TEACHER hits 1ST COMIC. HE whines, ad libs, "What did you hit me for? He's the one who said it," etc. HE sits and again plays with 2ND GIRL's leg.)*

TEACHER All right, _____, give us a sentence using the word "disaster."

1ST COMIC My girl backed into an airplane propeller. Disaster. *(TEACHER hits 1ST COMIC, knocks his wig off. HE reaches for wig, while TEACHER keeps hitting him. HE gets the wig back on, but crookedly.)* Wait until I screw my head back on.

TEACHER Now it's time for poetry.

1ST GIRL I love poetry.

2ND COMIC You're the type that would.

TEACHER _____, do you have one?

1ST GIRL *(jumping up to recite)*
THERE WAS AN OLD WOMAN
WHO LIVED IN A SHOE.
SHE HAD NO CHILDREN;
SHE KNEW WHAT TO DO.

1ST COMIC What's the address of that shoe? *(TEACHER hits 1ST COMIC.)*

TEACHER If you keep this up, _____, I'm going to keep you after school, take down your pants and spank your little bottom.

1ST COMIC You keep promising, but nothin' ever happens. *(TEACHER hits 1ST COMIC.)*

2ND COMIC *(raises hand)* Teach, can I go to the boy's room?

TEACHER Certainly, _____. You're excused.

1ST COMIC Hey, go for me, willya?

2ND COMIC Sure, pal. *(HE exits.)*

TEACHER Do you have one, _____?

1ST COMIC *(as 2ND GIRL grabs at him)* I had one when I came in.

TEACHER Let's hear it.

1ST COMIC MARY HAD A LITTLE WATCH;
SHE SWALLOWED IT ONE DAY.
FROM MILES THE PEOPLE CAME TO SEE
HER PASS THE TIME AWAY.
MARY TRIED AND TRIED AND TRIED,
THE TIME IT WOULDN'T PASS.
SO IF YOU WANT TO TELL THE TIME,
YOU LOOK UP MARY'S...

(TEACHER hits him.)

UNCLE. He's got a Rolex.

2ND COMIC *(returning)* Well, I went.

1ST COMIC Did you go for me?

2ND COMIC You didn't have to go. Teach, I've got a little one.

1ST COMIC I wouldn't boast about it.

2ND COMIC Here goes:
I KNOW A GIRL
FROM BOSTON, MASS.
SHE WADED IN WATER
CLEAR UP TO HER KNEES.

TEACHER That doesn't rhyme.

2ND COMIC It will when the tide comes in. *(1ST COMIC laughs, shakes 2ND COMIC's hand as if to congratulate him. TEACHER hits 1ST COMIC.)*

1ST COMIC I was six feet tall when I came in here.

TEACHER That brings us to the lesson of the day. _____, what's the difference between prose and poetry?

1ST COMIC That's easy. The pros stand on the corner.

TEACHER Well, obviously you don't know, so I'll have to explain.
MY GIRL RAN ROUND THE MULBERRY BUSH,
AND I RAN ROUND TO MEET HER.
THAT LITTLE GIRL WILL NEVER KNOW
HOW GLAD I WAS TO GREET HER.

1ST COMIC What's that?

TEACHER That's poetry. It rhymes.

1ST COMIC I see. Meet her, greet her. It rhymes. *(PUPILS agree.)*

TEACHER But if I were to say:
MY GIRL RAN ROUND THE MULBERRY BUSH,
AND I RAN ROUND TO MEET HER.
THAT LITTLE GIRL WILL NEVER KNOW
HOW GLAD I FELT THAT DAY.

1ST COMIC What's that?

TEACHER That's prose. You see, it doesn't rhyme.

1ST COMIC Oh, I see. Poetry rhymes, and prose doesn't. *(PUPILS nod assent.)* Is that all there is to it?

TEACHER That's all.

1ST COMIC May I give the class an example?

TEACHER Please do.

1ST COMIC MY GIRL RAN ROUND THE MULBERRY BUSH,
AND I RAN ROUND TO MEET HER.
SHE PULLED UP HER PETTICOAT,
AND I PULLED OUT MY...
Now, what do you want? Prose or poetry?

BLACKOUT

*The Lesson
of the Day*

A CLASSY PLACE
("My School Days Are Over")

Blackboard. Teacher's desk. Four desks for students. TEACHER enters ringing bell, followed by TWO GIRLS.

GIRLS Good morning, teacher.

TEACHER Good morning, girls. Where's little _____?

2ND COMIC *(entering)* Here I am, teach. Before class starts, may I ask a question?

TEACHER Certainly.

2ND COMIC Can an eleven-year old girl perform an appendix operation?

TEACHER Certainly not!

2ND COMIC *(showing scar on stomach)* See, you're going to have to put it back.

TEACHER Where's little _____?

1ST COMIC Here I am, teach. I'm sorry I'm late, but mother was late packing my lunch. Here it is. *(HE shows bag.)*

2ND COMIC *(grabbing bag)* Do you have nuts?

1ST COMIC No.

2ND COMIC Do you have dates?

1ST COMIC If I had nuts, I'd have dates.

TEACHER Quiet, children. It's time for our history lesson. Tell me, _____, what is Lincoln's Gettysburg Address?

2ND COMIC 1642 Walnut Street.

TEACHER That's enough of history. Now, it's time for social studies. Today we're going to examine familiar occupations. Tell me, _____, what are the duties of a gardener?

1ST COMIC A gardener is a man who takes his spade in his hand and goes out among the cabbages and peas.

TEACHER There's certainly enough of social studies. *(2ND COMIC whispers to 1ST COMIC, and a fight begins.)*

1ST COMIC No, he isn't.

2ND COMIC Yes, he is.

TEACHER What's the matter, boys?

1ST COMIC _____ says his father is better than my father.

2ND COMIC You bet he is. And my brother is better than your brother.

1ST COMIC No, he isn't.

2ND COMIC What's more, my mother is better than your mother.

1ST COMIC You've got me there. My father says the same thing.

TEACHER It's time for our English lesson. Tell me, _____, what is the difference between ignorance and apathy? Ignorance and apathy.

1ST COMIC I don't know, and I don't care.

TEACHER Right! Now, _____, use the word "denial" in a sentence.

1ST GIRL Certainly. "Denial." Cleopatra is the queen of denial.

TEACHER It's your turn, _____. Give me a sentence using the word "deceit."

2ND GIRL "Deceit." [1ST COMIC's] pants have a patch on deceit.

1ST COMIC De-pressing. *(TEACHER hits him.)*

TEACHER All right. _____, you're so smart. Use the words "honor" and "offer" in a sentence.

1ST COMIC That's easy. She offered her honor. He honored her offer. And all night long, it was on her and off her. *(TEACHER hits him again.)*

TEACHER That's all I can take of English. It's time for our poetry lesson.

1ST GIRL I love poetry.

TEACHER Do you have one, _____?

2ND COMIC She has one all right.

1ST COMIC She's showed it to us many times.

1ST GIRL JACK AND JILL WENT UP THE HILL;
EACH HAD A SHINY NEW QUARTER.
JILL CAME DOWN WITH FIFTY CENTS.
DO YOU THINK THEY WENT UP FOR WATER?

2ND COMIC I'm gonna have to get my father to raise my allowance.

1ST COMIC Hey, _____, do you want to come over to my house and play post office?

1ST GIRL That's a child's game.

1ST COMIC Not the way I play it.

TEACHER All right. _____, it's your turn. Do you have one?

1ST COMIC I have a little one.

2ND COMIC Don't boast about it.

1ST COMIC It's called "We were all out of firewood, so father came home with a load."

TEACHER *(sitting on desk, crossing her legs)* We don't want to hear that one. If you don't watch out, _____, you're going to flunk recess. Now, children. *(1ST GIRL raises her hand.)* What is it,_____?

1ST GIRL Teacher, I can see your ankles.

TEACHER That's a very rude observation, _____. You're suspended from class until tomorrow. Bring a note from your mother. *(1ST GIRL cries and leaves.)*

2ND GIRL Teacher, I can see your calf.

TEACHER What's got into you girls? You're suspended for three days. Bring a note from your mother. *(2ND GIRL exits.)*

2ND COMIC Teacher, I can see your thigh.

TEACHER That's it. _____, you're suspended for a week. *(2ND COMIC leaves, secretly delighted. 1ST COMIC gets up to follow him.)* Where are you going, _____?

1ST COMIC My school days are over.

BLACKOUT

There were more than fifteen stock courtroom scenes in Burlesque all based, according to Billy Hagan, on an inappropriately named blackface called "Irish Justice." The best of these sketches are "The Poetical Court," "After My Money," "Wise Child" and "The Westfall Murder Case."

I used material from all these scenes to create a courtroom scene for Miller and Rooney, but I took the plot from "The Westfall Murder Case."

THE COURT OF LAST RETORT
("The Westfall Murder Case")

POLICEMAN discovered in one.

POLICEMAN Hear ye. Hear ye. The Court of Common Pleas is now in session. Anyone with business before this court, make his presence known. No presents of less than twenty-five dollars accepted. All hail the Judge.

(Traveler opens to reveal courtroom with high Judge's stand. STRAIGHT MAN [D.A.] is discovered.)

D.A. All hail the Judge! All hail the Judge!

JUDGE *(1ST COMIC pops up from behind bench.)* Who said, "To hell with the Judge?" Have we any juicy cases today?

D.A. We have a case of bigotry, Your Honor.

JUDGE Bigotry? What's that?

D.A. A man is accused of marrying three wives.

JUDGE That's trigonometry. *(reaches below bench, brings out an old-fashioned telephone receiver)* Excuse me, I have a phone call. Hello, this is Judge _____. *(Phone rings late. JUDGE, D.A. and POLICEMAN look to the wings, as if to indicate that the Stage Manager has made an error. ALL pretend to be amused or disconcerted. JUDGE on phone)* Didn't I tell you never to call me at work? Haven't you hurt me enough? I never want to see you again. Never!

D.A. Who was that?

JUDGE My dentist. *(gavel)* What's the first case?

D.A. We have a murder case.

JUDGE It's about time! What's the case?

D.A. A woman did her husband in.

JUDGE What's the woman's name?

D.A. Westfall.

JUDGE Send in Mrs. Breastfall.

D.A. *(correcting him)* Westfall.

JUDGE I'm going to have trouble with that name.

(Enter PRIMA DONNA as MRS. WESTFALL in a sexy black dress.)

MRS. WESTFALL *(flirting with JUDGE)* Hello, Judgie.

JUDGE Would you like to come over to the Waldorf and talk it over for a few hours? *(HE puts his leg over the Judge's bench and starts to ride it.)*

D.A. Judge, stand on your dignity.

JUDGE It won't reach down that far. *(to MRS. WESTFALL)* Raise your right hand. Do you swear?

MRS. WESTFALL Constantly.

JUDGE Be seated. *(SHE wiggles into her seat, accompanied by appropriate noises from the DRUMMER.)* Wind that up and set it for eight o'clock.

POLICEMAN *(who clearly finds MRS. WESTFALL an exciting woman)* May I be excused, Your Honor?

JUDGE Yes, Phillips, go down and pound your beat. *(POLICEMAN exits.)* Now, Mrs. Asphalt, tell the court exactly how it happened.

MRS. WESTFALL Well, Judgie, it was just like this.

(SHE crosses her legs. The JUDGE drops his mallet, disappears from view, reappears at stage level through a swinging door in the Judge's stand. HE kneels down as if to pick up the mallet, and, of course, stares at her legs.)

D.A. What are you doing, Your Honor?

JUDGE I'm taking a closer look at this case.

D.A. Oh, I see. Are you scrutinizing the defendant?

JUDGE Not yet. But I may get lucky later on. *(HE hits her knee. It moves reflexively.)*

D.A. Look, Your Honor. When you hit it, it goes up.

(JUDGE turns and appears to hit himself in the groin with the mallet. HE turns around in pain as we hear the sound of birds twittering.)

JUDGE That's a beautiful diamond you're wearing.

MRS. WESTFALL Yes, it is, Your Honor. You've heard of the Hope Diamond?

JUDGE Who hasn't heard of the Hope Diamond?

MRS. WESTFALL Well, this is the Westfall Diamond. It comes with a curse.

JUDGE What's the curse?

MRS. WESTFALL Mr. Westfall.

D.A. *(as JUDGE returns to bench)* Now, Mrs. Westfall, tell this court exactly what happened on the night in question.

MRS. WESTFALL Well, I was fast asleep in my boudoir at 3:00 in the morning when my husband burst in without touching the knocker.

JUDGE Without touching the knocker? Must be a leg man.

MRS. WESTFALL Do you know what that man wanted me to give him?

JUDGE I've got a pretty good idea.

MRS. WESTFALL A hot home-cooked supper!

JUDGE Did you give it to him?

MRS. WESTFALL Certainly not!

JUDGE Well, I can't blame you. Who's gonna lay it on the table at three o'clock in the morning? I bet that made him mad.

MRS. WESTFALL Oh, it did, Your Honor. He called me vile names. Then we began to wrestle. First I was on top. Then he was on top. Then I was on the bottom, and he was on top. Then he was on the bottom, and I was on top. Then we both wound up on top. *(Her gestures complement her words.)*

JUDGE I never tried that position. What happened then, Mrs. Foreplay?

D.A. *(correcting him)* Westfall.

MRS. WESTFALL He whipped out a gun.

JUDGE *(mock outrage)* What?

MRS. WESTFALL He whipped out a gun.

JUDGE Was it a big one?

MRS. WESTFALL Oh, about this big. *(suggests with her hand gestures that the gun is very large indeed)*

JUDGE He belongs in the book of records. What kind of gun was it?

MRS. WESTFALL A repeater.

What happened then, Mrs. Foreplay?

JUDGE *(with a knowing look)* Ah! A repeater!

D.A. Yes. A repeater! You have a repeater, don't you, Judge?

JUDGE No, all I've got is a little single shot...little puff of smoke comes out. What happened then, Mrs. Fishballs?

D.A. Westfall.

MRS. WESTFALL I grabbed his gun.

JUDGE *(mock outrage)* What?

MRS. WESTFALL I pulled on it, and we fought. I pulled on it, and we fought. I pulled on it, and we fought. And finally, the gun went off.

JUDGE Well, that was bound to happen. You pull on a gun long enough, it's gonna go off. *(to D.A.)* What have you got to say to all of this, Dudley?

(As D.A. speaks, JUDGE flirts with MRS. WESTFALL.)

D.A. Your Honor, ladies and gentlemen of the jury, there sits a woman who lies. She claims her husband came home at three A.M. The man worked hard all day. After work he stopped in for a drink—perhaps two or even three. But was he drunk? No, I say, Your Horseship. That man was...

JUDGE *(after a short take)* Back it up. What did you call me?

D.A. I said, "Your Worship."

JUDGE You sure there wasn't a little horse in there somewhere?

D.A *(neighing)* Nay! Nay!

JUDGE That sounds a little hoarse. Who cares?

D.A. Who cares? *(JUDGE bangs gavel.)* Who cares if it was three o'clock in the morning? He simply asked for something to eat. But did he get it? No! I say, Your Horseship.

JUDGE That'll be enough horseship out of you. *(HE bangs gavel.)*

D.A. That woman is guilty, and I demand that you give her the full extent of the law.

JUDGE Who are you to demand?

D.A. I'm the District Attorney.

JUDGE I'm Justice.

D.A. Justice who?

JUDGE Just as good as you are. Now, Mrs. Lipstick, tell us exactly where you shot your husband.

MRS. WESTFALL *(pleased tone)* I shot him between the green beans and the asparagus.

D.A. There, Your Honor. You see. She's guilty. She admits it. She shot her husband between the green beans and the asparagus.

JUDGE Well, it could have been worse.

D.A. How?

JUDGE If she'd shot him two inches lower...

D.A. Yes?

JUDGE She'd have caught him right in the zucchini.

MRS. WESTFALL *(rising)* Your Honor! Your Honor! Are you going to give me a stiff sentence?

JUDGE If I get a good night's sleep, you can depend upon it. Now, I know the pain you're suffering, Mrs. Breakwind, but before I pass sentence, do you have anything to say in your own defense?

MRS. WESTFALL Yes, Your Honor, I just want to say that my husband was a mean man.

JUDGE & D.A. *(echoing angrily)* Mean!

MRS. WESTFALL He used to beat me.

JUDGE & D.A. Beat!

MRS. WESTFALL He used to chase me around the room.

JUDGE & D.A. Chase!

MRS. WESTFALL Rip off my clothes.

JUDGE & D.A. Rip!

MRS. WESTFALL Using and abusing my body.

JUDGE He should have been hung!

MRS. WESTFALL Oh, he was!

BLACKOUT

A doctor's office is a wonderful venue for a Burlesque scene, since it is a dangerous and potentially sexy place. After all, in low comedy the stakes should be high, and where are they higher than in an examining room.

Billy Hagan often performed a scene called "The Doctor Shop," in which he played a bewildered plumber mistaken for Dr. Plummer, the eccentric heart specialist. Tools in hand, he has come to repair a leaky valve in the bathroom. Instead, he is invited to scrutinize a beautiful, nearly naked patient to see if she has a leaky heart. "What a break for a plumber," he says, masking his delight from the straight man but letting the rest of us share it. I shall never forget Billy's high squeaky voice when he said that line and the little smile that hinted at profound delights.

To me, that moment was the distilled essence of Burlesque humor. Billy's tramp gave silly hope to all of us. Perhaps we, too, might be mistaken for a Doctor Plummer, or draw five aces in a poker game or win the favors of a luscious lady by waving a magic poppy underneath her nose. Not all our aspirations are heroic, and we should not despise those shabby comforts that sometimes lead to (threadbare) joy.

In memory of Billy, I am including "Dr. Plummer" in this collection. Alone of all these sketches, I have made no effort to adapt it or improve it. Without the genius of Billy's personality, it seems on paper a little tired. But it was delightful when he performed it.

DR. PLUMMER
("The Doctor Shop")

STRAIGHT (as DOCTOR) and SOUBRETTE (as PATIENT) are discovered in a Doctor's office. HE is listening to her heart action through his stethoscope.

DOCTOR I must say, Miss _____, yours is a most unusual case. For the first time in my long years of practice, I'm baffled. But don't be discouraged. I have sent for Dr. Plummer, the world's most eminent heart specialist. I've never met the man, and I hear he's very eccentric.

PATIENT *(alarmed)* Eccentric?

DOCTOR Yes, but there's no cause for alarm. Despite his little peculiarities, he is a brilliant physician. He'll find out what's wrong with you and fix you up in a jiffy.

PATIENT When do you expect him?

DOCTOR At any moment.

    (Big bang offstage. Door has been slammed. Enter the COMIC as a PLUMBER. HE sees the PATIENT and whistles.)

DOCTOR Whom do I have the pleasure of meeting?

PLUMBER I'm the plumber.

DOCTOR Oh, Doctor Plummer. *(shakes hands)*

PLUMBER No, the plumber.

DOCTOR *(still shaking his hand)* I understand. Dr. Plummer.

PLUMBER You don't understand. I'm the plumber. *(PLUMBER breaks away from the handshake.)* What do you think this is? A pump handle? *(sees PATIENT, tips his hat)* Hello, baby, I'm the plumber...the plumber...plum, plum, plumber.

DOCTOR You're eccentric.

PLUMBER And you're screwy as hell. *(DOCTOR pats PLUMBER's butt* *and pushes him toward PATIENT.)* Cut out the monkey business. I want to go to work. I'm waiting for my boy, and if he don't show up, I get paid anyway. I'm a union man. Where's the leak?

DOCTOR Right over there. *(points to PATIENT)*

PLUMBER What? The lady's got a leak?

DOCTOR Yes, a leaking heart.

PLUMBER What do I know about leaking hearts? I fix sinks, bathtubs and sewer pipes.

DOCTOR *(flirtatiously)* My, how eccentric!

PLUMBER *(indicating DOCTOR)* I'm sure of that one. Stop fooling around. I want to go to work.

DOCTOR Well, get to it. Go over and scrutinize that young lady.

PLUMBER Scrutinize her. I can do that?

DOCTOR Certainly.

PLUMBER *(indicating AUDIENCE)* In front of all these people? Cheese and crackers.

DOCTOR I scrutinize everyone that comes into this room.

PLUMBER I was afraid of that. I'd better get out of here.

DOCTOR Too late. I've scrutinized you already.

PLUMBER You have? Where was you?

DOCTOR Right here.

PLUMBER Where was I?

DOCTOR *(indicating door)* Over there.

PLUMBER Six to five you can't do it again.

DOCTOR I'm scrutinizing you right now. *(PLUMBER cuts through air with hand to see if anything invisible is happening. HE is satisfied that nothing is going on.)*

PLUMBER Sixteen to five.

DOCTOR What are you talking about? Scrutinize her! Diagnose her case!

PLUMBER Stick my nose in the case.

DOCTOR Go over and examine her.

PLUMBER Examine her? What do I know about examining her? I'm a plumber, you son of a biscuit. Plumber.

DOCTOR This is getting out of hand, Dr. Plummer. Examine her.

PLUMBER If I examine her, I'll get a slap in the face.

DOCTOR No. No. That's what she's here for.

PLUMBER She's here for that purpose?

DOCTOR Yes.

PLUMBER What kind of place did I wander into?

DOCTOR I want you to use your stethoscope on her.

PLUMBER My what?

DOCTOR Stick it in your ear.

PLUMBER *(hollers)* What am I? A contortionist?

DOCTOR *(hands PLUMBER his stethoscope)* Here. Use this on the young lady.

PLUMBER Is this what you were talking about?

DOCTOR Yes.

PLUMBER I get the damnedest ideas.

DOCTOR Use it on her.

PLUMBER *(PLUMBER holds rubber end of stethoscope out straight, then lets it drop.)* What the hell good is this? *(lets it drop again)* From here down, it's dead. I use this on the young lady?

DOCTOR Yes.

PLUMBER My, how times have changed.

DOCTOR Examine her from top to bottom.

PLUMBER Everywhere?

DOCTOR Don't miss a spot.

COMIC *(aside to AUDIENCE)* What a break for a plumber! All right, if you say so, I will. I don't know what this is all about, but I won't argue anymore. Young lady, please take off all your clothes.

PATIENT Shall I, doctor?

DOCTOR Yes, it's perfectly all right now.

PLUMBER Certainly. That's the only way I can stick my nose in the case.

(PATIENT goes upstage, takes off her dress, hangs it on the hall tree. Wearing only a bra and panties, SHE comes downstage and stands next to the PLUMBER.)

DOCTOR Do you think you can find it?

PLUMBER I'll find it all right. Even in the dark, I can feel my way to it. Are you sure everything is going to be fine?

DOCTOR Oh, yes.

PLUMBER Nobody is going to interfere?

DOCTOR Certainly not.

PLUMBER I don't want to get her all steamed up and have some sucker come in and spoil it.

DOCTOR Do you think you can go through with it?

PLUMBER I'll go through it. Then I'll come back and go through it again. I might go through it three or four times, you never can tell. *(HE turns and sees the PATIENT undressed.)* Cheese and crackers. May I start?

DOCTOR Yes.

PLUMBER With the...

DOCTOR Stethoscope.

PLUMBER Ice pick. *(With the ear pieces of the stethoscope, HE heads for PATIENT's breast.)* You lay it on there, and I'll nip it to death. *(to DOCTOR)* There's enough there for the three of us.

DOCTOR Three of us?

PLUMBER Sure. Me, you and then me again. *(hands stethoscope to DOCTOR)* Here. Hold this. I can do better with nothing in my hand.

DOCTOR Take the action of the heart. *(PLUMBER puts his ear near PATIENT's right breast.)* No, that's the wrong side. Look, I'll demonstrate.

PLUMBER Not on me, you won't.

DOCTOR It'll just take a second.

PLUMBER That's what they all say.

DOCTOR *(singing to tune of "SIDEWALKS OF NEW YORK")*
WRONG SIDE *(pinches PLUMBER's right chest)*
RIGHT SIDE *(left chest)*
ALL AROUND THE DIAPHRAGM *(rubbing his stomach with a circular motion)*
HEY! HEY!
RIGHT SIDE *(left chest)*
WRONG SIDE *(right chest)*

ALL AROUND THE DIAPHRAGM *(rubbing stomach)*
HEY! HEY!

PLUMBER I'm beginning to wonder about him. He does that a little too well.

DOCTOR *(very butch)* Now, wait a minute. We're acting up here. You're giving them the wrong idea. Why, when I leave the theatre, there's likely to be twenty guys at the stage door waiting for me.

PLUMBER Twenty-one.

DOCTOR Why?

PLUMBER I'll be there.

DOCTOR Back to business.

PLUMBER Well, miss, there's nothing for it. I'm going to have to take the action of your heart. *(HE sings, imitates the DOCTOR's business, except HE doesn't actually pinch the PATIENT's breasts. HE does, however, rub her stomach. HE says in a steamy voice.)*
WRONG SIDE,
RIGHT SIDE,
ALL AROUND THE DIAPHRAGM.
HEY! HEY!
(to DOCTOR) You ain't got the steam on in here, have you?

DOCTOR No.

PLUMBER *(voice becoming so choked, HE almost doesn't finish)*
RIGHT SIDE,
WRONG SIDE,
ALL AROUND THE DIAPHRAGM.
HEY! HEY!

DOCTOR *(patting PLUMBER's butt)* I'll help you.

PLUMBER Looks to me like you're helping yourself. *(PLUMBER leans into PATIENT's breast.)* Oh, that tickles.

DOCTOR At last, doctor. I can see your technique.

PLUMBER Is that damn thing hanging down again? I'll have to get a vest. *(holds tightly to PATIENT)* Say "ah," mama.

PATIENT Ah.

PLUMBER Oh, Adam. Look down on your son Cain and make him able.

PATIENT Ah. *(TROMBONE PLAYER in band raises his instrument.)*

PLUMBER *(to TROMBONE PLAYER)* Put that damn thing down, Harry. I'm not through yet.

PATIENT Ah.

PLUMBER Ah.

(PLUMBER and PATIENT repeat the "Ahs," with the PLUMBER becoming more excited each time. Finally, SHE is alarmed. HE chases her to the hall tree. HE takes her dress and hat from hall tree, puts them down his pants and whistles.)

PLUMBER She's in bad shape. I'll have to operate.

PATIENT Oh, doctor, operate quick. Operate quick. *(grinds and bumps; PLUMBER grabs her and pulls her to the door.)*

DOCTOR Where are you going?

PLUMBER To the operating room.

DOCTOR You'd better take my instrument.

PLUMBER No. No. I've got my own instrument.

BLACKOUT

The lame joke that concludes "Dr Plummer" illustrates one of the problems of adapting these sketches for Broadway consumption. Often the authentic Burlesque bits end with a whimper not a bang. And during the preparation of *Sugar Babies*, my constant challenge was to find a concluding punch line that was not anticlimactic.

The problem is particularly acute with respect to scenes that developed out of improvisations, as I suspect "Dr. Plummer" did. Someone, maybe Billy Hagan, invented the premise, and the scene was padded out from there.

However, a few of the traditional sketches were written not improvised. Among the anonymous creators of Burlesque bits were Aaron Hoffman, who began his career in minstrel shows and Billy K. Wells, a Ziegfeld hanger-on, who wrote not only for the low comics, but also contributed pieces to sophisticated revues.

"The Transformer," the funniest of all the doctor scenes, may have been written by Hoffman or Wells. Milton Berle acted in a version of it and claimed it as his own; but certainly he was not the first author. Still, whoever was responsible, there's no doubt that the piece had an author. It wasn't created collectively. The sketch is a fully developed seven-minute farce, as carefully constructed as Feydeau's *The Ribadier System*, a piece which it resembles.

"The Transformer" has a few risky elements. It is not what might be called politically correct. The references to stuttering may seem insensitive, and even though homosexual jokes were a staple of Burlesque, popular opinion has turned against their use.

But as Thomas Dekker once said, "There is no music without frets." "The Transformer" is hilarious when performed and worth the risk. This scene, incidentally, is the only full-length doctor sketch which I adapted for any version of *Sugar Babies*. But I made constant use of medical blackouts, seven of which are included here as a coda to this section.

2ND COMIC and 1ST COMIC meet in one, possibly in front of street drop.

1ST COMIC Hello, _____. You look a little under the weather.

2ND COMIC I'm having a bad day. I slept right through my nap. I missed the whole thing.

1ST COMIC Come with me.

2ND COMIC Where are you going?

1ST COMIC My girlfriend works in a doctor's office. Maybe he'll give you a tonic to pep you up.

2ND COMIC You go on. I don't trust doctors.

1ST COMIC Doctors are very smart.

2ND COMIC Oh, yeah?

1ST COMIC Oh, yeah. I'll give you an example. Last month, I had a little proctological problem—you know the kind I mean.

2ND COMIC The rubber cushion kind?

1ST COMIC Yep. And it got so bad I decided to go to my proctologist. He shares an office with a shrink. They call themselves "Odds and Ends." But my mother stopped me.

2ND COMIC Why was that?

1ST COMIC She said that when she was growing up in Cleveland, the native Indians—you know, the Cleveland Indians—had a folk remedy that would save me the cost of an expensive specialist.

2ND COMIC Really?

1ST COMIC She said I should make an internal application of tea leaves. The tannic acid, she said, would give me instant relief.

2ND COMIC Did it?

1ST COMIC No. When I shoved the tea leaves up there, they caused the most intense agony I ever felt in my life. Now, I had to go to the proctologist, who commenced to look at me through a proctoscope like this...*(indicates squinting through small lens)* I said, "Doctor, doctor, what do you see?"

2ND COMIC Yes?

1ST COMIC He said, "You're going to take a long trip. You're going to meet a tall dark stranger." You see, these doctors know a thing or two. Come on. I'm just going to have a fast slap and tickle with my girlfriend. Her boss will set you straight.

2ND COMIC No, thanks. I'm going to the Can of Nails Saloon.

1ST COMIC Why?

2ND COMIC I'm going to drink to forget.

1ST COMIC Forget what?

2ND COMIC I don't remember.

(THEY exit, ONE L., the OTHER R., as traveler draws to reveal a doctor's office. A Rube Goldberg machine C., flanked by two chairs. Two thick wires with six-inch handles extend from each side of the machine. This machine, at rise, is covered by a curtain. NURSE is on the telephone.)

NURSE Dr. Cutter's office. Nurse Bedpan speaking. Someone said what? If Dr. Cutter treats you for liver trouble, you'll die of indigestion? That's a lie. If he treats you for liver trouble, you'll die of liver trouble. *(SHE slams phone down as DOCTOR enters.)*

DOCTOR Well, nurse, what's the news from the hospital? How's Harry Walker, the poor little boy who swallowed the quarter?

NURSE No change yet.

DOCTOR How's Mrs. Gilmore? Has she taken my advice and stopped smoking?

NURSE Yes, she has.

DOCTOR That's good.

NURSE Not really. She burst into flames last Tuesday.

DOCTOR Sometimes nothing can be done. But never mind, nurse. These minor setbacks shouldn't bother us. *(pulls cloth off machine)* Wait until the public hears about my revolutionary new machine—the Disease Transformer.

NURSE Disease Transformer? How does it work?

DOCTOR I'm glad you asked. A patient comes here with an illness. It doesn't matter what the illness is. I place the patient in this chair...*(indicates R. chair)*...and put the handle in his hand. I'll pull this master switch, and the disease passes from the body of the patient through these conductors into this dummy. Where's the dummy?

NURSE Dummy?

DOCTOR I told you to order me a dummy yesterday. Don't tell me you forgot?

NURSE *(nodding yes and no simultaneously)* No...yes...no. It's in the next room.

DOCTOR Good. Go get it and place it in the chair. And don't forget, nurse, if business improves, I'll slip you a nice big bonus later on. Now, don't forget the dummy. *(HE exits R.)*

NURSE Dummy? Dummy? Where on earth am I going to get a dummy?

(1ST COMIC sticks his head in from proscenium and whistles.)

1ST COMIC Are we alone? Here I am, sweet thing. Papa wants a morning kiss.

NURSE Oh, _____, I warned you not to come here. The doctor's very strict. If he catches us together, I'll be fired. *(1ST COMIC kisses her. SHE is aroused. A bell rings off L.)* That must be a patient. Where can I hide you? *(HE tries to get under her skirt.)* No, that's the first place he'll look. I have it. Sit in this chair. *(grabs him by his suspenders and snaps him into chair)* You can be the dummy.

1ST COMIC Dummy?

NURSE Yes. You're perfect for the part. No one will know the difference. *(enter 1ST PATIENT)*

1ST PATIENT I wish to see the d...d...d...

NURSE Doctor?

1ST PATIENT Physician.

NURSE Oh, doctor, a patient to see you.

DOCTOR *(entering)* What seems to be the problem?

1ST PATIENT I st...st...st...

DOCTOR Stutter?

1ST PATIENT Stammer.

DOCTOR Do you stutter very often?

1ST PATIENT Only when I t...t...t...

DOCTOR Talk?

1ST PATIENT Speak.

DOCTOR What do you do for a living?

1ST PATIENT I used to be a radio an...n...n...

DOCTOR Announcer?

1ST PATIENT Commentator. But now I work in a b...b...bird store.

DOCTOR What do you do in the bird store?

1ST PATIENT I teach p...p...parrots how to talk.

DOCTOR *(speaking very quickly)* Young man, your worries are over. Sit in this chair and hold this handle. *(as PATIENT sits)* Your ailment will be carried through these conductors into the body of this dummy. *(notices COMIC)* Dear me, that's the saddest excuse for a dummy I've ever seen. *(to PATIENT)* Are you ready?

1ST PATIENT Yes. Give it the j...j...j...

DOCTOR Juice?

1ST PATIENT Current. *(DOCTOR pulls switch. Machine explodes, lights up, etc.)* Why, doctor, it's miraculous. I don't stutter any more. How much do I owe you?

DOCTOR I'll send you a bill. *(1ST PATIENT exits L. DOCTOR starts to exit R.)* I told you, nurse, this machine will make my fortune. And when it does, I'll slip you that nice big bonus. *(HE exits.)*

NURSE Come on, Butch. You have got to get out of here. *(1ST COMIC jumps up. HE tries to talk, but finds HE can't. Whistles, then hits himself on the head.)* What's the matter, sweetheart?

1ST COMIC I can't t...t...t...

NURSE Talk?

1ST COMIC Converse. *(HE starts to go.)* Show me to the d...d...d...

NURSE Door?

1ST COMIC Exit. *(Bell rings.)*

NURSE Too late. *(NURSE snaps him into chair by his suspenders as 2ND PATIENT enters. The 2ND PATIENT [female] is scratching herself energetically.)* You wish to see the doctor?

2ND PATIENT Oh my, yes. Oh my, yes. *(DOCTOR enters.)*

Oh, doctor. I itch all over....

NURSE Well, here he is.

DOCTOR What seems to be the trouble, miss?

2ND PATIENT Oh, doctor. I itch all over. I itch all over.

DOCTOR Young lady, don't be rash. Sit in this chair and hold the handle. Your ailment will be carried through these conductors into the body of that dummy. *(noticing 1ST COMIC again)* My goodness, that's an ugly dummy. Send it back, nurse, and get another one. *(to 2ND PATIENT)* Are you ready?

2ND PATIENT Oh, yes. This itch is terrible. I really pity that dummy. *(1ST COMIC winces.)*

DOCTOR Did that dummy move?

NURSE Oh, no.

DOCTOR Because if he did, the doctor will find another place to stick this handle. *(1ST COMIC freezes.)* Here goes! *(same business as before with the machine)* How do you feel now?

2ND PATIENT Wonderful! You've cured my itch!

DOCTOR Well, come into the office, and you can cure mine. *(HE and 2ND PATIENT exit. 1ST COMIC starts scratching furiously.)*

NURSE What's the matter, sweetheart?

1ST COMIC I can't t...t...t...

NURSE Talk.

1ST COMIC Take any more of this. *(The bell rings. HE starts to go.)*

NURSE *(trying to push him back)* Now, Butch.

1ST COMIC You go f...f...f...

NURSE *(shocked)* Butch!

1ST COMIC Find yourself another dummy. *(Bell rings. SHE snaps him back as 3RD PATIENT, a NANCE, enters.)*

NURSE Can I help you?

NANCE I hardly think so. I want to see the doctor.

NURSE *(as DOCTOR enters)* Here he is.

DOCTOR What's the matter, sir?

NANCE Well, I know you'd never guess it from my appearance, but sometimes I feel like a woman.

DOCTOR Is that so?

See you later, sweet thing.

NANCE Yes, and I'm tired of being girlish. I want to be a man, doctor. I want to be a handsome brute like you.

DOCTOR Well, sit in this chair. *(NANCE does so. DOCTOR puts handle in his hand.)*

NANCE Oooh. Where did you come from, big boy?

DOCTOR Now squeeze it tight.

NANCE Oh, I know how to squeeze it.

DOCTOR No, no. You see, this is my disease transformer. Your complaint will pass through these conductors into the body of that dummy. *(looking at 1ST COMIC)* That dummy is all lopsided. It isn't even human looking.

NANCE *(going over to 1ST COMIC)* Oh, I don't know, doctor. He looks pretty virile to me. Tell me, do they make these dummies complete in every respect?

DOCTOR In every respect.

NANCE They never leave an inch or two out?

DOCTOR Never. *(NANCE pinches 1ST COMIC's cheek.)*

NANCE See you later, sweet thing.

    (NANCE sits in chair. DOCTOR pulls switch; same business as before.)

DOCTOR How do you feel now?

NANCE *(suddenly very butch)* Wonderful, doctor. As soon as I pay you, I'm going home and beat up the biggest bully on the block. *(HE exits; DOCTOR accompanies him to door.)*

DOCTOR It won't be long, nurse. Soon I'll be slipping you that big bonus. *(exits)*

NURSE Quick, give me a kiss, and then go.

1ST COMIC I'd rather k...k...kiss the d...d...doctor.

    (Enter a YOUNG WOMAN. NURSE snaps 1ST COMIC back into his seat.)

NURSE What can I do for you, miss?

YOUNG WOMEN I'm going to have a baby.

1ST COMIC *(jumping up from chair)* Oh, no, you don't.

BLACKOUT

...beat up the biggest bully on the block.

STRAIGHT, as DOCTOR, wheels on a large cart on which we can see three human brains in glass containers of bubbling preservative. PATIENT (2ND or 3RD COMIC) enters with him.

DOCTOR Now, Mr. Wimple. I must warn you that a brain transplant is not without its element of risk.

PATIENT Risk?

DOCTOR Yes. It varies, but I would estimate the mortality rate as somewhere between ninety-seven and ninety-eight percent.

PATIENT I don't care, doctor. If I can't have this transplant, I'll never get my promotion.

DOCTOR Well, then, the first thing you have to do is decide which brain you want.

PATIENT You mean I have a choice?

DOCTOR Oh, yes, indeed. *(pointing to containers)* Now, the brain in the first container belonged to the former president of Harvard University. *(consulting a card)* That brain will cost you five thousand dollars installed. *(The PATIENT nods.)* The second brain was once the property of a Nobel prize-winner. *(looks at card)* That runs about ten thousand dollars with all the moving parts. *(Again the PATIENT nods.)* Now, the third one is a real beauty. It belonged to one of the writers of this show. *(consulting card)* It's a bargain at thirty-five thousand dollars.

PATIENT Now, wait a second, doctor. Five grand for the president of Harvard, ten thousand dollars for a Nobel prize-winner, and you're telling me that the brain of a writer is worth thirty-five G's? How come?

DOCTOR Well, that last brain's never been used.

BLACKOUT

102

FINALLY A NUDE SCENE
("On Top of Mine")

Lights up. Doctor's office. DOCTOR on phone.

DOCTOR Yes, this is Doctor Syringe's office. What are your symptoms? You say you're having trouble breathing? Well, I can stop that. You want an appointment? *(looks at appointment book)* I can give you an appointment two weeks from Tuesday. You might be dead by then? Well, you can always cancel.

BEAUTIFUL PATIENT *(entering)* Ah, doctor.

DOCTOR Yes, Miss _____, what can I do for you?

BEAUTIFUL PATIENT I want a thorough physical examination.

DOCTOR Yes, of course. Please take off all your clothes.

BEAUTIFUL PATIENT Oh, doctor, I couldn't possibly undress in front of you. I'm too shy.

DOCTOR That's perfectly understandable. I tell you what we'll do. I'll turn the light off. You take off your clothes and tell me when you're finished.

BEAUTIFUL PATIENT That's very thoughtful.

(DOCTOR switches off light. We are in complete darkness. We hear a rustle of clothes in the dark.)

BEAUTIFUL PATIENT *(in dark)* I suppose you think I'm very silly, doctor.

DOCTOR *(in dark)* Not at all, miss. I admire modesty in a woman.

BEAUTIFUL PATIENT Well, I've taken off all my clothes. Where shall I put them?

DOCTOR Right over here on top of mine.

BLACKOUT

HARSH TREATMENTS
("Prickly Heat")

Doctor's office. NURSE discovered by hospital screen.

COMIC Nurse! Nurse! I've come to see the doctor.

NURSE You'll have to wait your turn. Meanwhile, read this release. *(HE sits by nurse's desk.)*

DOCTOR *(sticking head through door R.)* Oh, Sister Washrag.

NURSE Yes, doctor?

DOCTOR When you get a chance, send out for another ten-gallon can. That next patient has a lot of blood. *(HE exits.)*

NURSE Yes, doctor.

COMIC Maybe I'm not as sick as I thought I was. *(HE starts to go.)*

NURSE Come back here. *(gives him paper)* Raise your right hand and repeat after me. I solemnly swear...

COMIC I swallowed a hair. What's this for?

NURSE Didn't you read the release? You're swearing to hold us blameless in case of death or disfigurement.

COMIC Oh, I see. If I die, it's my fault.

(A scream. From behind the screen the 1ST PATIENT enters. His hand covers his left ear. HE starts out toward R. proscenium.)

1ST PATIENT I have erysipelas [ear-i-sip-i-lus], so the doctor cut off my ear.

(HE exits R. A second scream of pain from behind the screen. Enter 2ND PATIENT limping with a bandage on his foot. HE starts out R. COMIC stops him.)

COMIC Hey, bud. What's the matter with you?

2ND PATIENT I had ptomaine poisoning, so the doctor cut off my toe. *(HE exits, limping.)*

COMIC Erysipelas, ear? Ptomaine poisoning, toe? *(starts to exit)* See you later, nurse.

NURSE What's the matter with you?

COMIC I've got prickly heat.

BLACKOUT

Nurse! Nurse!

A POULTRY PROBLEM
("Eggs")

In one, at L. proscenium STRAIGHT (as PSYCHIATRIST) at desk. COMIC standing, WOMAN sitting.

WOMAN Doctor, we're desperate. Since you're the most eminent psychiatrist in the city, we thought you could help us.

PSYCHIATRIST. What seems to be the trouble? *(HUSBAND cackles like a chicken and moves his arms as if they were wings.)*

WOMAN My husband thinks he's a chicken. *(another cackle)*

PSYCHIATRIST How long has he suffered from this delusion?

WOMAN For five years.

PSYCHIATRIST Five years? Why did you wait so long to consult me?

WOMAN We needed the eggs.

BLACKOUT

COMPLICATIONS
("Absent-Minded Doctor")

MAN wheeled in from operating room by NURSE.

1ST COMIC Where am I? Where am I?

NURSE Don't try to talk. You're just coming out of the ether.

1ST COMIC What was I doing with ether?

NURSE You were unconscious. The doctor found a thousand dollars in your pocket, so he took your appendix out. *(enter 2ND COMIC)* And, look, here's a friend come to visit you. *(SHE exits.)*

2ND COMIC *(slapping 1ST COMIC on stomach)* So you had your appendix out? Does it hurt very much?

1ST COMIC That isn't helping it any.

2ND COMIC Who was your doctor?

1ST COMIC Doctor Slicem.

2ND COMIC Not old Bumblehead Slicem?

1ST COMIC Why do they call him that?

2ND COMIC Six months ago he performed a liver transplant—and left his saw inside the patient. Had to cut him up again to get it out.

1ST COMIC Oh, dear. Well, I guess it can happen to anyone.

2ND COMIC Last week he was taking out some gallstones...

1ST COMIC And he left his saw inside?

2ND COMIC *(laughs)* Of course not.

1ST COMIC *(also laughing)* I didn't think so.

2ND COMIC He left his rubber gloves in the guy—had to cut him open again to get them out. *(HE laughs uproariously. 1ST COMIC joins in weakly.)*

1ST COMIC Forgetful cuss, isn't he?

    (Enter DOCTOR. HE looks under bed and elsewhere in the room.)

1ST COMIC Doctor, I'm feeling much better. When can I go home?

DOCTOR Now where's my umbrella? I know I left it somewhere.

BLACKOUT

Now where's my umbrella?

SOCIALIZED MEDICINE
("Specimen Blackout")

S.L. lights up. PATIENT (COMIC) with 10-quart specimen filled to the brim. DOCTOR (STRAIGHT MAN) at desk. Papers and telephone on the desk.

DOCTOR *(reading from paper)* Well, Mr. _____, that is the healthiest specimen I have ever tested in my life. The sugar content is ideal; the percentage of salt is perfect.

PATIENT May I use your phone to call my wife?

DOCTOR Certainly. Is she nervous waiting for the news?

PATIENT No. My wife doesn't know the meaning of the word "fear." In fact, there are lots of words she doesn't know the meaning of. *(into phone)* Is that you, Edna? Yes, I'm all right. And you're all right. The children are all right. Your mother's all right. Even the horse is all right.

BLACKOUT

ACCIDENTS OF BIRTH
("Maternity Ward")

Four beds with foot toward audience, charts, etc.; in other words, we are in a typical maternity ward. Each bed has a PATIENT. Enter DOCTOR, followed by NURSE.

DOCTOR *(to 1ST GIRL)* Good evening, Miss _____, how are you feeling?

1ST GIRL Fine.

DOCTOR And when do you expect your baby?

1ST GIRL March 12th.

DOCTOR *(to 2ND GIRL)* Good evening, Miss _____, how are you feeling?

2ND GIRL Fine.

DOCTOR And when do you expect your baby?

2ND GIRL March 12th.

DOCTOR *(to 3RD GIRL)* And when do you expect your baby?

3RD GIRL March 12th. *(DOCTOR starts toward 4TH GIRL.)*

NURSE Don't disturb her, doctor. She was restless last night, and this is the first time she's had some sleep all day.

DOCTOR Does anyone know when this young lady expects her baby?

1ST GIRL No, doctor. She wasn't on that picnic with us.

BLACKOUT

M any Burlesque performers began their professional careers in tent shows or carnivals. So, not surprisingly, many stock Burlesque scenes dramatize the pleasures and dangers of the Midway.

One of the oldest of all the standard sketches is "The African Dodger." The Mutual comics who played the scene were white, but, as the name suggests, the piece was originally a blackface minstrel act.

I adapted this hoary skit for a revue about baseball called *Diamonds*, which was produced by Louis Scheeder and directed by Harold Prince at Circle-in-the-Square downtown.

I first saw it performed in 1950 by the late Mac Dennison, who, by that time, had been dodging the baseballs for more than thirty-five years.

THE DODGER GAME
("The African Dodger")

S.R. a ticket booth. S.L. a board with a hole in it backed by some curtains. Sign above board reads: "BIG BASEBALL GAME. HIT THE TARGET AND WIN A PRIZE." Enter COMIC with bedraggled baseball uniform on and a cigar in his mouth.

STRAIGHT What's the matter, young man?

COMIC I came here to get a tryout with the White Sox, but they wouldn't let me in the gate.

STRAIGHT They have no sense of humor in there.

COMIC That's right.

STRAIGHT What are you going to do now?

COMIC Go back to my old woman. There's a problem though.

STRAIGHT Oh?

COMIC She wants me to go to work.

STRAIGHT Ridiculous.

COMIC You know as well as I do, there's no money in work.

STRAIGHT That's a good cigar you're smoking.

COMIC I always smoke good cigars.

STRAIGHT You do?

COMIC That is, when I can get them.

STRAIGHT A good cigar is hard to get.

COMIC I had a hard time getting this one.

STRAIGHT You did?

COMIC I had to walk four blocks for it. I thought the guy was never going to throw it away.

STRAIGHT I think I can solve your cigar problem. You want a baseball job; I'll give you a baseball job.

COMIC I've got experience. Last year, I was the trainer for a girl's softball team. But I was fired.

STRAIGHT Why?

COMIC I rubbed them the wrong way. But that's in the past. Do you work for the White Sox?

STRAIGHT In a way. You see, I run a concession outside the park. It's called The Dodger Game.

COMIC How does it work?

STRAIGHT Well, the people come along here, and I sell them these balls, three for a nickel. A fellow sticks his head through the hole. The aim of the game is to hit that fellow on the head.

COMIC You want me to sell the balls?

STRAIGHT No. I want you to stick your head through the hole.

COMIC Not my head. *(starts to go)*

STRAIGHT Are you yellow?

COMIC No, that's just a liver condition.

STRAIGHT Listen, there's no danger at all. *(HE has a ball in his hand.)* This is all they throw. *(drops ball; it's metal)*

COMIC That's all they throw?

STRAIGHT That's all.

COMIC You don't want me. You want my brother.

STRAIGHT Why?

COMIC My mother don't care what happens to him.

STRAIGHT There's nothing to worry about. *(takes out a cloth cap)* This is a protector. You put this protector on your head. When the people throw balls at you, they bounce off the protector.

COMIC But what makes the balls bounce off the protector? I reiterate: what makes the balls bounce off the protector? I'll tell you what makes the balls bounce off the protector. My head underneath the protector. Take back your protector.

STRAIGHT I see you're a little nervous. Suppose we use a ball like this? *(bounces a rubber ball to COMIC)* A ball like that won't hurt.

113

COMIC Not unless they put nails in it.

STRAIGHT There are no nails in this game.

COMIC Are you sure?

STRAIGHT Word of honor.

COMIC I'll take the job. *(HE crosses to board, puts head through hole.)* How do I look?

STRAIGHT Great.

COMIC I feel great.

STRAIGHT You won't for long. *(to gathering crowd)* The Dodger Game is open, ladies and gentlemen. Balls are three for five; hit the little man on the head. Knock his brains out and win a big prize.

COMIC *(comes out from board)* Don't say knock his brains out. They might take you at your word.

STRAIGHT They can't knock out what you haven't got.

COMIC Leave my brains out of this game.

STRAIGHT I'm leaving them out. Hit the little man on the head and win a baby doll. *(SOUBRETTE enters R., sees the COMIC, starts to laugh.)*

SOUBRETTE Look at that silly little man.

STRAIGHT Hit the funny man in the head, young lady, and win a big prize.

SOUBRETTE I never threw a ball in my life, but I'll have a try.

(STRAIGHT hands her three balls. SHE throws the first ball high above his head. COMIC laughs. SHE throws the second ball way to the right and the third way to the left. SHE laughs and exits.)

COMIC Hey, boss, did you see me duck them?

STRAIGHT Damn right I did.

COMIC Boy, I live in this game.

STRAIGHT Yes, and you're going to die in this game.

COMIC I don't like the way you read that last line.

STRAIGHT I mean that you will be in this game so long that you'l die of old age.

COMIC Let's improve things. From now on, have them throw nothing but hard balls.

(Enter WALTER JOHNSON in baseball uniform.* HE walks up to STRAIGHT, shakes hands. COMIC begins to quake.)

STRAIGHT Well, if it isn't my old friend, Walter Johnson. How are you doing, Walter? *(COMIC is trying to sneak away. STRAIGHT sees him.)* Hey, where are you going?

COMIC It's time for lunch.

STRAIGHT You can't go now. We have a customer.

JOHNSON By the way, how is the boy I hit on the head yesterday?

STRAIGHT That boy died this morning.

JOHNSON Well, that's not my fault.

STRAIGHT Certainly not. I furnish the boys, and you throw the balls.

COMIC *(whistles to STRAIGHT)* Can I see you a minute?

STRAIGHT Why, certainly.

COMIC Is this who I think it is?

STRAIGHT Yes, but don't worry. He'll miss you ninety-nine times out of a hundred. *(JOHNSON throws three balls very fast—right through the hole.)* Didn't I tell you he'd miss?

COMIC He missed everything but the hole.

(A TOUGH enters with two bricks in his hand, throws one onto the floor and starts winding up with the other brick. COMIC sees this, starts running and hides behind ticket booth. STRAIGHT takes the brick from the TOUGH's hand.)

STRAIGHT There are no bricks in this game.

JOHNSON Hey, what's the big idea? I was here first.

TOUGH But I'm going to throw first. *(JOHNSON and TOUGH ad lib argument.)*

STRAIGHT Boys, boys. Let me settle this. Johnson, you throw first, and when you get through...*(to TOUGH)*...Dutch, here, can step in and finish him off. O.K.?

TOUGH Sounds good to me.

STRAIGHT How about you, Johnson?

JOHNSON Sounds good to me, too.

---

*Or Randy Johnson or Roger Clements.

COMIC Well, someone has to kill me off.

TOUGH Make sure you stun him. Because if you don't, I'll come back and paralyze him for sure.

COMIC Get that murderer out of here.

STRAIGHT *(as JOHNSON warms up)* Are you ready?

COMIC Yes, I'm ready.

STRAIGHT All right, get in the hole.

COMIC I've got a better idea. I'll stand over here. I can duck 'em better.

STRAIGHT You can what?

COMIC I can duck 'em better.

STRAIGHT If you stand over there, he will shower you with them.

COMIC I don't care if he rains them on me.

(JOHNSON throws, and about fifty baseballs fall to the stage almost hitting the COMIC.)

BLACKOUT

The next three scenes were part of the repertory of Bert Carr, the first Burlesque comedian I ever worked with. Bert, like Billy Hagan, was a sophisticated and skillful comic who, despite other offers, chose to continue in Burlesque even in its sad final days. Although he had a face like a Hellenistic comedy mask (when he removed his false teeth), Bert was a very gentle, understated comedian. He played a good-natured but greedy clown, always hungry. His tag-line, "you gotta eat," was worked into all conversations, often in a cunning and round-about way.

Although Bert was an excellent serious actor—he had worked with Boris Thomashefsky at the Yiddish Art Theatre—there was no pathos in his comic style. In another century what a Harlequin he would have made!

All in all Bert was one of the most versatile performers I ever saw. He was a wonderful comic victim, which is why "Five Aces" suited him so perfectly. But he could also be hard-edged, as in unsentimental knockabout farces like "The Celery Scene."

A NICE SOCIABLE GAME
("Five Aces")

1ST COMIC and 2ND COMIC meet in one in front of a street drop.

1ST COMIC Well, if it isn't Sober Sam. You look a little under the weather, Sam.

2ND COMIC What kind of place is this? I saw a door marked WOMEN; I went in, and there wasn't a damn one. Besides, I had a bad day at the races.

1ST COMIC I'm sorry to hear it.

2ND COMIC I bet a hundred bucks on "I Don't Know," and I don't know what happened.

1ST COMIC What horse did you bet on?

2ND COMIC "I Don't Know."

1ST COMIC Don't you know the horse's name?

2ND COMIC Sure, I know the horse's name.

1ST COMIC Well, what's his name?

2ND COMIC "I Don't Know."

1ST COMIC You just said you *do* know.

2ND COMIC I do know.

1ST COMIC Then what is it?

2ND COMIC "I Don't Know."

1ST COMIC I asked the horse's name.

2ND COMIC And I told you.

1ST COMIC What did you tell me?

2ND COMIC "I Don't Know."

1ST COMIC Do you take me for a fool?

118

2ND COMIC No, but I could be mistaken.

1ST COMIC Of course, I didn't go to Yale or Harvard, but just the same, I'm a college graduate.

2ND COMIC What college is that?

1ST COMIC Vaseline College. I just slipped in and out. The horse has a name?

2ND COMIC Of course, he has a name.

1ST COMIC Now suppose that horse is coming into the home stretch.

2ND COMIC Right.

1ST COMIC You want to root for him.

2ND COMIC Sure, I want to root for him.

1ST COMIC You want to call out something to make that horse run faster.

2ND COMIC You bet I do.

1ST COMIC Then what do you call out?

2ND COMIC "I Don't Know," "I Don't Know," "I Don't Know!"

1ST COMIC Oh, "I Don't Know" is the name of the horse.

2ND COMIC Yes. Why did you misconstrue me?

1ST COMIC I don't know.

2ND COMIC Maybe racing's not my game.

1ST COMIC What is it then?

2ND COMIC Poker. And while I think of it, there's a game tonight down at my lodge.

1ST COMIC What lodge is that?

2ND COMIC The Sons of the Mystic Possum.

1ST COMIC You belong to that?

2ND COMIC Yes. I rank as Supreme Highness and Most Exalted Possum Potentate. They call me "Your Fragrance."

1ST COMIC You must be head man in that lodge.

2ND COMIC No, I just joined. That's the lowest rank.

1ST COMIC And they play poker?

2ND COMIC Every Friday night. I have guest privileges.

1ST COMIC I'll go on one condition.

2ND COMIC What's that?

1ST COMIC We cheat.

2ND COMIC Now you're talking. You pitch in and do your part, and I'll pitch in and do my part.

1ST COMIC And if we don't pitch in and do our parts, we won't have a part to pitch in.

(THEY exit as the travelers draw to reveal the Inner Sanctum of the Possums. A poker table C. with three chairs. Underneath the table is a wire basket. A chorus of Possums is singing the anthem for the lodge. 1ST COMIC and 2ND COMIC enter. 2ND COMIC exchanges elaborate ritual greeting with his lodge brothers.)

2ND COMIC Hello, Brother Pewter. Hello, Brother Jonah. This here is _____. He's here to play some poker.

PEWTER (CHARACTER MAN) _____?

2ND COMIC He's the toughest man north of Baxter Street.

1ST COMIC Damn right I am.

PEWTER Well, he'd better be tough if he's going to play poker here tonight. Big Bullets is out of jail again, and he's on his way over here looking for a game.

1ST COMIC Big Bullets from Baltimore? The same Big Bullets who shot his grandmother when she tried to hide a quarter from him?

PEWTER That's right.

1ST COMIC The same Big Bullets who beat the brains out of Irish Jack McCloskey for stealing ten cents from him on a policy bet?

PEWTER The very same.

1ST COMIC Is he a member of this lodge?

JONAH (JUVENILE) He's a member of any lodge he wants to be.

2ND COMIC You ain't afraid of him, are you, _____?

1ST COMIC Afraid? Me afraid? Why, if I had Big Bullets here, I'd rip him limb from limb...*(BIG BULLETS [STRAIGHT], a wicked-looking man with an eye patch, has entered unseen by 1ST COMIC. HE draws a big gun. The other LODGE BROTHERS sneak away and exit.)*...I'd take his left leg with my left hand and his right leg with my right hand, and I'd pull him apart like a turkey's wishbone. I'd...

(BULLETS shoots gun between 1ST COMIC's legs.)

BULLETS Well, why don't you do something?

120

1ST COMIC I think I did.

BULLETS Boys, all those stories about me, they ain't true. I'm not a hard man. I want to be friends. How about a nice quiet game of poker?

1ST COMIC *(turning to go)* Oh, no.

BULLETS *(pointing gun at back of 1ST COMIC's head)* I say yes.

1ST COMIC Well, I say...*(turns, looks right into gun)*...yes?

(THEY go to table and sit. 1ST COMIC, L. of table; BULLETS, R.; and 2ND COMIC, C.)

BULLETS Good. Now this is going to be a nice sociable game. *(HE slams gun on table.)*

2ND COMIC Well, if it's going to be sociable, I'll play. *(takes hatchet from behind chair, slams it on table)*

1ST COMIC I might as well be sociable, too. *(takes brick from behind chair and slams it on table)*

BULLETS To prove it's going to be sociable, I brought my own cards.

1ST COMIC *(to 2ND COMIC)* How can we lose?

BULLETS Now, gentlemen, there's going to be no cheating in this game. *(picks up gun)* The first little bedbug that I catch cheating—I don't want to mention no names—but I'm going to shoot his brown hat right off his head. *(HE looks at 2ND COMIC during this speech until the very end when HE suddenly turns to 1ST COMIC.)*

1ST COMIC There ain't a lot of brown hats here. *(HE is wearing the only brown hat.)*

BULLETS Now, gentlemen, I will deal the cards...*(HE deals.)*...and remember, the first man I catch cheating...*(HE makes gesture as if shooting pistol.)*...I will make a new hole in his head.

1ST COMIC *(shows cards to audience one by one)* The first guy he catches cheating, he's coming to make a new hole...*(As HE mutters these words, BULLETS is dealing. 1ST COMIC gets an ace and then a second ace.)* Not bad for a start. A five and a six. *(HE starts to hum. HE gets a third ace. Not having a poker face, HE smiles and hums louder. HE gets a fourth ace. His humming is ecstatic. HE gets a fifth ace. Now, HE knows HE's in trouble. HE looks nervously at the gun and hatchet.)*

2ND COMIC *(to 1ST COMIC)* Have you got openers?

1ST COMIC I've got openers all right.

2ND COMIC Well, so do I. And being a sport, I'll open for ten cents.

BULLETS (*rising, outraged*) What?!

1ST COMIC (*rises, his voice pulsing with drama*) Shame on you! Shame on you! I brought you up since you were a baby. I tried to make a man of you, to teach you right from wrong. I took you around the world, introduced you to famous people like Big Bullets here. He invites us as a great favor to play poker, and you open the pot for ten cents. Shame on you! We don't play for no dimes!

BULLETS (*hitting table*) Certainly not!

1ST COMIC (*sitting down*) We'll play for a nickel.

BULLETS (*with gun*) We play for dollars.

2ND COMIC I'll bet ten dollars. (*puts money from his pile in center of table*)

1ST COMIC (*showing cards again*) Well, to tell you the truth, Bullets, I don't have nothing, but just to be a sport, I'll stay for ten dollars. (*puts money from his pile in C.*)

BULLETS Good. Bullets bets, too. (*puts up money; to 2ND COMIC*) How many cards to you want?

2ND COMIC (*tough*) How many can I get?

BULLETS (*looks up, puts gun in 1ST COMIC's face*) What's that?

1ST COMIC Shut up before he kills me.

BULLETS How many cards do you want?

2ND COMIC Four.

BULLETS You'll take three and like it.

2ND COMIC I'll take three, but I won't like it. (*BULLETS gives him three.*)

BULLETS (*to 1ST COMIC*) Well, now, termite, how many cards do *you* want?

1ST COMIC I don't want any.

BULLETS You don't want any?

1ST COMIC (*looking intently at cards*) I've got too damn many now.

BULLETS This is draw poker, and you have to draw cards. (*points gun at 1ST COMIC's head*)

1ST COMIC I said I'll take...(*turns and sees gun*)...three. (*throws three cards on floor, looking forlornly at them*)

BULLETS (*deals him three*) Very sensible. Very sensible.

1ST COMIC If I were sensible, I wouldn't be in this game. (*HE turns over cards one by one, mugging on each. Needless to say, each is an ace.*)

BULLETS (*to 2ND COMIC*) How much you bet?

2ND COMIC I'll bet fifty dollars. (*puts money on pile*)

BULLETS I'll see your fifty and raise you two hundred.

2ND COMIC I'll see your two hundred and raise you five hundred. (*HE takes money from BULLETS' pile, while the latter is occupied with his cards.*)

1ST COMIC (*seeing 2ND COMIC take BULLETS' money*) This is going to be a nice sociable game. I'll see that five hundred and raise you a thousand. (*takes money from 2ND COMIC's pile, puts it on his own pile, then slams elbow on it*)

BULLETS I'll see that thousand and raise you five thousand. (*puts money on the pile*)

2ND COMIC What do you mean five thousand? Don't be a piker. I'll raise you ten thousand.

(*An elaborate piece of business here. There is a wire basket under the table. 2ND COMIC maneuvers it into position under front of table with his legs, shoves money off edge of table into basket, pulls it back toward him, reaches down and takes the money. One torn bill remains in the center of the table.*)

1ST COMIC (*looking up*) I see that...(*notices that money is gone; picks up torn bill*)...the depression is on. Well, I'll see that last bet and raise you fifteen thousand.

BULLETS And I raise you fifteen thousand.

2ND COMIC What do you mean? I raise you twenty thousand. (*keeps talking and scoops money into basket as before*)

1ST COMIC (*kissing his brick; to 2ND COMIC*) Hey, pal, do you have a couple of aspirin?

2ND COMIC No. Why?

1ST COMIC In a minute you're going to have a helluva headache. (*slaps brick on table*)

2ND COMIC I raise you ten thousand more.

1ST COMIC That's pretty risky, ain't it, Bullets?

BULLETS I can't lose.

1ST COMIC (*looking at cards and rearranging them*) How do you know?

BULLETS My fairy godfather is looking out for me. You have a fairy godfather, don't you, woodlouse?

1ST COMIC No, I've got an uncle I'm not too certain of. (*putting money on pile*) O.K., I'll see that ten thousand and raise you ten thousand more.

2ND COMIC Here's my ten, and here's ten more.

> (*Same business as before, but this time when 2ND COMIC pushes the bills over the edge of the table, 1ST COMIC catches them with his hat before they can reach the basket. 1ST COMIC slams his hat on his head. 2ND COMIC pulls the basket back, feels for money, finds none. HE looks over the front of the table, doesn't see money. HE looks at 1ST COMIC and hits table with the hatchet.*)

You're going to look damn funny with one hand.

1ST COMIC Come on, let's bet it all. (*BOTH agree and do so. BULLETS rises and points at 2ND COMIC.*)

BULLETS What have you got?

2ND COMIC I ain't got bluffing. I was only nothing. I mean, I ain't got nothing. I was only bluffing.

BULLETS (*to 1ST COMIC*) What have you got?

1ST COMIC (*points to gun and points it to his head*) I've got a headache.

BULLETS (*menacingly*) No. What have you got in the cards?

1ST COMIC Nothing. You win.

BULLETS (*laughs, walking down to the foots*) Thought you could get the better of Bullets, did you? I eat beetles like you for breakfast. (*HE laughs again.*)

2ND COMIC Hurry up. Take the money, and let's get the hell out of here.

> (*1ST COMIC scoops up money; BOTH run L. BULLETS notices them trying to escape, shoots over their heads. BOTH stop.*)

1ST COMIC I think he wants us.

BULLETS So you laugh behind my back!

1ST COMIC We didn't laugh.

BULLETS You know why I'm called Bullets?

1ST COMIC No.

BULLETS *(takes cartridges from his pocket, offers them to 1ST COMIC)* Eat them!

1ST COMIC No, no, please.

BULLETS You eat those damn bullets, or I shoot you. *(puts two bullets in 1ST COMIC's mouth, then makes him eat a third one)* And here's one for dessert. *(1ST COMIC rises.)* Now, I'm going to get a nice long rope. Then I'll come back and hang you.

2ND COMIC I see you like eating bullets.

1ST COMIC I ate them, but I didn't like them. Boy, they're a little heavy on the stomach. *(bends over and rubs stomach; a big explosion)* _____, did you shoot?

2ND COMIC No.

1ST COMIC Well, I didn't shoot.

2ND COMIC If you say so, _____.

1ST COMIC I thought I heard a shot. *(rubs stomach again, another loud explosion; to 2ND COMIC)* Are you sure you didn't shoot?

2ND COMIC No.

1ST COMIC And I didn't shoot.

2ND COMIC If you say so.

1ST COMIC Well, somebody shot. *(HE walks away R. as BULLETS enters with rope. 1ST COMIC's back is to him, and 1ST COMIC bends over as if to belch.)*

BULLETS Now I kill you. *(1ST COMIC hits his stomach again. Another loud shot. BULLETS grabs his stomach and falls.)* He got me. *(HE dies.)*

2ND COMIC Say, pal, did you shoot?

1ST COMIC Shoot, hell. I backfired.

BLACKOUT

THE BIGGERMAKER
("Celery Scene")

Enter in one STRAIGHT MAN and COMIC behind him. The scene then goes to an interior dining room. Props needed are: round dining table, 4 chairs, 4 large plates, 4 knives, 4 forks, 4 spoons, salt and pepper shakers, 9 stalks of celery each show (long stem), 1 box of Uneeda Biscuits, 1 banana each show, 1 ear trumpet for deaf man, 1 imitation roast chicken, 1 tray, 1 small bowl, 1 large long platter.

STRAIGHT *(to COMIC)* What are you following me for?

COMIC I want a drink, and you always buy my drinks.

STRAIGHT I've only got fifty cents, just enough for one drink.

COMIC That's all I want is one drink. And I'm hungry. I gotta eat.

STRAIGHT I've got an idea. We'll have plenty to drink and enough to eat.

COMIC How?

STRAIGHT Tonight I'm going to my girl's house to ask her father for his consent to marry. No doubt he'll ask me some questions. I want to make a good impression so I'll take you along. You'll be my secretary.

COMIC I suck whose strawberry?

STRAIGHT No! Secretary. Now, for example, if he asks me if I have a car, I'll say I have a Model-T. That's where you come in. You say, "Oh, no, he has a Packard Saloon." In other words, you make it bigger for me.

COMIC You're going to get married, and I've got to make it bigger for you? That's a helluva job. I'm a biggermaker.

STRAIGHT Yes.

COMIC When do I start as a biggermaker?

STRAIGHT Right now.

COMIC When do I eat?

STRAIGHT I'll tell you when to eat.

COMIC That's hard work being a biggermaker, and when a man works hard, he uses up a lot of energy, and when a man uses up a lot of energy, what happens?

STRAIGHT What?

COMIC You gotta eat.

STRAIGHT I'll tell you when to eat.

COMIC Don't worry. You can depend on me. I'm a good biggermaker. I belong to the biggermaker's union. I got a union book in my pocket. You know what it says on page 37?

STRAIGHT What?

COMIC You gotta eat.

STRAIGHT Come along with me. You'll get plenty to eat.

(*BOTH exit L. Curtain opens to reveal dining room. CHARACTER MAN and GIRL discovered.*)

GIRL Father, tonight my boyfriend is coming to ask you for my hand in marriage. I hope you'll consent.

CHARACTER (*who is deaf and has an ear trumpet*) Eh?

GIRL I said my boyfriend is coming tonight to ask for my hand in marriage. I hope you'll consent.

CHARACTER We'll see; we'll see. (*knock on door*)

GIRL Come in.

STRAIGHT (*enters L.*) Hello, sweetheart.

GIRL Hello, dear, I want you to meet my father.

STRAIGHT Hello, Mr. Beertaster.

CHARACTER Eh?

GIRL You'll have to talk louder.

STRAIGHT I'm glad to meet you.

CHARACTER Sit down; sit down. Young man, I understand you want to marry my daughter. Now, how much money do you earn a week?

STRAIGHT Fifty dollars a week.

CHARACTER Well, that may be all right for one, and it may be good for two, but suppose you have children?

STRAIGHT We won't have any children.

CHARACTER What makes you so sure you won't have children?

STRAIGHT Knock wood, we've been lucky so far. *(COMIC enters L.)*

COMIC What kind of joint is this? The elevator is broke. I walked up four flights.

STRAIGHT O.K., take it easy. You know what I'm here for.

COMIC Yeah, I gotta make it bigger for you. You know what I'm here for?

STRAIGHT What?

COMIC You gotta eat.

STRAIGHT I want you to meet my fiancée. This is my secretary.

COMIC *(embraces GIRL)* How do you do? You gotta eat.

STRAIGHT I want you to meet my future father-in-law. This is my secretary, Mr. Beertaster.

COMIC Hello, Mr. Billpaster.

CHARACTER Eh?

COMIC What's the matter with him?

CHARACTER You'll have to talk louder.

COMIC Didn't I meet you in Cincinnapolis last week?

CHARACTER Never was in Pennsyltucky in all my life.

COMIC Neither was I. Must have been two other guys.

CHARACTER Ha! Ha! Ha! *(As CHARACTER takes a cracker into his mouth, HE spits out the cracker.)* Serve the dinner.

MAID *(entering R.)* Oh, Miss Beertaster, the cook just quit, and there isn't a thing to eat in the house.

GIRL Well, just pretend you're serving the food. *(MAID exits R.)* Oh, honey, we're going to have clams.

MAID *(enters)* Clams, clams, clams, clams. *(SHE exits.)*

GIRL Oh, look, my clams are smiling at me.

STRAIGHT My clams are winking at me.

COMIC My clams are hiding from me.

CHARACTER Ha! Ha! Ha! *(COMIC hits CHARACTER with celery.)*

STRAIGHT What's the matter with you?

COMIC Where do you see clams?

STRAIGHT You ate them.

COMIC I did?

STRAIGHT You ate half a dozen clams.

COMIC Maybe I did. *(HE belches.)* Yep, I ate them.

GIRL Now we're going to have soup.

MAID *(enters)* Soup, soup, soup, soup. *(SHE stumbles, spills imaginary soup on COMIC, exits.)*

COMIC Who spilled that soup on me? *(hits CHARACTER with celery)*

GIRL Now, dear, we are going to have chicken. By the way, what part of the chicken do you like?

STRAIGHT I like the breast.

COMIC That son of a gun ain't been weaned yet.

STRAIGHT What part of the chicken do you like?

COMIC If it's all the same to you, I'll take duck.

CHARACTER Say, did you ever see a duck duck a duck?

COMIC No, but I saw a goose goose a goose. *(CHARACTER laughs; COMIC hits him.)*

CHARACTER Young man, you owe me an apology.

COMIC Oh, go to hell.

STRAIGHT Go ahead and apologize.

COMIC O.K. I accept your apology.

CHARACTER I accept your apology. Una. *(throws out hand with one finger extended)*

COMIC Due. *(two fingers extended)*

CHARACTER Tre. *(three fingers extended)*

COMIC Cuatro. *(four fingers extended)*

CHARACTER Cinque. *(five fingers extended)*

COMIC *(putting hand in pocket)* He called me a stinker. I'll kill him.

GIRL Don't shoot! Don't shoot!

STRAIGHT I appeal.

COMIC *(pulling banana from pocket)* I'll peel it myself.

CHARACTER What's that?

COMIC A banana.

CHARACTER I like bananas.

COMIC Take some. (*As CHARACTER reaches for banana, COMIC hits him with celery.*)

CHARACTER Daughter, leave the room. There are a few questions I want to ask your friend.

GIRL (*exiting*) I'll see you in the parlor.

COMIC I'll see you in the basement. (*MAID enters with chicken, places it on table, then exits.*)

CHARACTER Now, young man, have you any money?

STRAIGHT I have a few dollars.

COMIC He's got millions.

CHARACTER Eh?

COMIC He's got millions. Millions.

CHARACTER Eh?

COMIC He's got piles.

CHARACTER I had them, too. I got rid of them. (*COMIC hits him.*) Have you got a house?

STRAIGHT I've got a small bungalow.

COMIC He's got a mansion.

CHARACTER Eh?

COMIC He's got a mansion. He's got a hundred rooms and a thousand baths.

CHARACTER Eh?

COMIC He's got a bathhouse. (*hits CHARACTER again*)

CHARACTER Have you got any water around the house?

STRAIGHT I've got a small lake.

COMIC He's got a lagoon.

CHARACTER Eh?

COMIC He's got a spittoon. (*hits him again*)

CHARACTER Have you got a yacht?

STRAIGHT I've got a rowboat.

COMIC He's got a wassel.

CHARACTER Eh?

COMIC He's got a wassel, a wassel.

CHARACTER How dare you call me a weasel?

COMIC I didn't call you a weasel. I said a wassel. A wassel and a weasel are two different things. A wassel starts with a "we" and a weasel starts with a "wubble you."

CHARACTER I see. I see.

COMIC If you can see half as well as you hear, you're cockeyed.

CHARACTER Do you own any land?

STRAIGHT I've got a lawn around the house.

COMIC He's got plenty of land. He's got a forest.

CHARACTER Eh?

COMIC You know where Central Park is in New York?

CHARACTER Yes.

COMIC You know where Lincoln Park is in Chicago?

CHARACTER Yes.

COMIC You know where [name of park] is in [LOCAL CITY]?

CHARACTER Yes.

COMIC Well, what about it?

CHARACTER What about what?

STRAIGHT You asked him three questions.

COMIC He can't answer one. I'll prove it to you. What are you doing the fourth of July?

CHARACTER Nothing.

COMIC I'll be able to use you.

CHARACTER What for?

COMIC Punk.

CHARACTER Bah, bah, bah!

COMIC Bah yourself, you old fool.

CHARACTER That calls for a fight. You called me a fool.

COMIC Take it easy; you'll fall down.

STRAIGHT He didn't call you a fool. He said he likes to play pool.

CHARACTER Oh, I used to play pool in a competition.

COMIC I used to play pool in a poolroom.

CHARACTER I'd like to play you a game.

COMIC All right. I'll show you I'm a regular guy. I'll spot you eight balls and bank the last shot. *(STRAIGHT coughs.)*

CHARACTER Young man, you've got a bad cough.

COMIC Cough? Hell, he's got consumption.

STRAIGHT *(takes COMIC downstage)* All right, you did enough damage. You ruined everything for me. Now, I'm going to get even. You see this chicken? Whatever you do to this chicken, I'll do to you. If you cut off the right wing, I'll cut off your right arm. If you cut off the left leg, I'll cut off your left leg. Whatever you do to this chicken, I'll do to you.

CHARACTER That goes for me, too, you whippersnapper. Whatever you do to that chicken, I'll do to you.

COMIC Whatever I do to this chicken, you'll do to me? Well, if I must I must. *(HE kisses the rear of the chicken.)*

BLACKOUT

"The Gazeeka Box" is an ancient Burlesque sketch that exists in many versions. The one printed here derives from the variations which Bert Carr played first on the Mutual Circuit and finally in my production of *The Naughty Nifties* at the Pittsburgh Playhouse in 1963. I had forgotten the finish to the scene. (The final stage direction in my thirty-two year old script simply reads, "Business to be explained.") Fortunately Peter Larkin, whose memory clearly is better than mine, supplied what I had forgotten.

Al Anger, on the old Hirst Circuit, played "The Gazeeka Box" as a "double victim" scene (see p. 21), complete with a second comic to whom Anger sold the box after having been conned by the straight man.

In all its incarnations the sketch derives from what we might call the Pygmalion fantasy. What man wouldn't want a beautiful and pliable Galatea who owed her existence to him, and who, if called upon to do so, would be only too happy to stroll into the garden "to see where the squirrels bury their nuts"? The Burlesque Galateas, of course, were not so pliable as one might hope.

The etymology of the word "Gazeeka" is not easy to trace. The tramp clown was never a skillful communicator. Any nonsense word could dazzle him. Indeed, any innocent word of more than two syllables could create an aggressive misunderstanding. Witness the way in which "scrutinize" is used in "Dr. Plummer" or "predicament" in "Who Dyed."

THE GAZEEKA BOX

As the CHORUS finishes the number, the STRAIGHT enters dressed as a sultan, followed by TWO MEN who wheel out a giant cabinet with a draw curtain. A sign on the top of the cabinet says SULTAN'S GAZEEKA BOX.

STRAIGHT Well done, and now my slaves, I expect a friend of mine. He's very excitable and mustn't see you. *(GIRLS exit as COMIC enters.)* Ah, hah.

COMIC Don't stop me. I lost it. I lost it.

STRAIGHT Lost what?

COMIC My love persuader. It came from the tomb of an Egyptian king. It looks like a peanut. I call it King Tut's nut. You wave it under a girl's nose, and she falls madly in love with you.

STRAIGHT King Tut's nut, eh? Where did you lose it?

COMIC *(pointing left)* Over there.

STRAIGHT Then why are you looking for it over here?

COMIC There's more light over here.

STRAIGHT Forget your old Egyptian peanut. I have something much better than that. I am the Great Marvello, master of magic. Would you like to see my gazeeka?

COMIC Why would I want to see your gazeeka?

STRAIGHT I possess the most marvelous gazeeka the world has ever known.

COMIC What's so marvelous about it?

STRAIGHT Kings have raved about it. Queens have swooned at it.

COMIC Dogs have barked at it.

STRAIGHT I carry my gazeeka in a box.

COMIC *(aside)* Boy, that's some gazeeka.

STRAIGHT Here it is. My powerful gazeeka box from which I bring forth my beautiful gazeekas.

COMIC You have more than one?

STRAIGHT Watch in amazement, oh useless one. *(chants)* Oh, Master, Master. Look down on your seventh son of a seventh son. Bring forth a gazeeka. Put the magic words in my mouth. Fee, fi, fo, fum—and here we have a beautiful gazeeka. *(STRAIGHT opens the curtain to the box. A beautiful GIRL in scanty costume is revealed. COMIC approaches and offers to touch her.)* No, no, don't touch her. The gazeeka is made of clay.

COMIC Who makes her?

STRAIGHT The Great Sculptor in the Sky. He gently forms the clay, then puts the gazeekas against the wall to dry, and he says, "You're done. You're done. You're done." *(HE twists thumb at GIRL's navel.)*

COMIC *(looking behind GIRL)* Boy, this gazeeka is well done.

STRAIGHT *(taking her down front)* Come, my dear gazeeka. I'll take you into the garden and show you the buttercups making butter. *(exits with GIRL)*

COMIC *(approaching box)* Well, I've got to get me a gazeeka. *(chants)* Oh, Master, look down on your seventh son of a seventh son and bring forth a gazeeka. Put the magic words in my mouth. Fee, fi, fo, fum—and here we have…*(opens curtain)*…not a damn thing. I'd better see what's in there. *(HE steps into the box. STRAIGHT enters and grabs COMIC by the seat of his pants.)* Hey, do you play for the Yankees?

STRAIGHT What do you mean?

COMIC You're in centerfield!

STRAIGHT What are you doing in there?

COMIC I'm trying to get a gazeeka.

STRAIGHT Only the certified owner of this powerful gazeeka box can get a gazeeka.

COMIC And you are the owner?

STRAIGHT That's right.

COMIC Where's that first gazeeka?

STRAIGHT I left her in the garden watching the buttercups make some butter.

COMIC I'll see you later.

STRAIGHT Where are you going?

COMIC I'm going to show here where the squirrels bury their nuts. *(HE exits.)*

STRAIGHT *(chants)* Oh, Master. Oh, Master. Look down on your seventh son of a seventh son. Bring forth a gazeeka. Fee, fi, fo, fum, and here we have a…*(HE opens the curtain. COMIC is standing there.)* How did you get in there?

COMIC The Great Sculptor put me here. You said only the owner of the gazeeka box can get a gazeeka?

STRAIGHT *(pulling COMIC out of the box and closing the curtain)* That's right. Just watch. Oh, Master. Oh, Master. Look down on your seventh son of a seventh son. Bring forth a gazeeka.

COMIC *(peeking into box)* Hey, cancel that order. There's one in there already.

STRAIGHT Fee, fi, fo, fum. And here we have a beautiful gazeeka.

> *(HE draws the curtain. A beautiful GIRL is standing there. ALL come down to the footlights.)*

GIRL Where am I?

COMIC You're in the old Howard Theatre.*

GIRL My, how strange it looks!

COMIC Well, they cleaned it up this morning.

GIRL *(to STRAIGHT)* What are you?

STRAIGHT I'm a man.

GIRL What's a man?

COMIC *(aside)* Oh, this is a damn shame.

STRAIGHT Well, a man is…well, you are a woman and I'm a man, and there's a difference.

COMIC Hooray for the difference!

GIRL Well, if you are a man, *(looks at COMIC)* what is that?

COMIC *(with an exasperated expression)* Huh! I'm a man, too.

GIRL *(pointing to his pants)* What is that?

COMIC That's trousers.

---

*Or in whatever theatre the show is currently playing.

...and bring forth a gazeeka.

GIRL What are trousers for?

COMIC They cover a multitude of sins.

GIRL *(pointing to pocket)* What is that?

COMIC A pocket.

GIRL What's a pocket for?

COMIC To keep your hands in.

GIRL What have you got in your hand?

COMIC *(taking roll from pocket)* Money.

GIRL Give me the money.

COMIC She's no gazeeka.

> *(Music plays. GIRL dances around the COMIC, massaging his chest and arms. COMIC gets steamy and gives her his money.)*

GIRL *(pointing to COMIC's watch fob)* What's that?

COMIC That's a watch.

GIRL Give me the watch.

COMIC Oh, no! I gave you that money. You're not getting the watch. *(Music. GIRL dances, again makes love to the COMIC.)* Here's the case; I'll give you the works tomorrow. Come on, baby. *(starts to lead GIRL off)*

STRAIGHT Where are you going?

COMIC I'm going out to the garden to show her the crocodiles playing with their little crocks.

STRAIGHT That's my gazeeka. Get one of your own.

COMIC Then sell me the box.

STRAIGHT Sell you this powerful gazeeka box? Never!

COMIC I'll give you five dollars for it.

STRAIGHT You twisted my arm. *(COMIC gives STRAIGHT money. STRAIGHT exits with GIRL U.C.)*

COMIC Oh, Master. Oh, Master. Look down on the seventh son of a seventh gun and bring forth a gazeeka. See, mi, blow gum, and here we have a…

> *(HE opens the curtain. In the box, very ugly WOMEN and MEN— STAGE HANDS, MUSICIANS, etc., who chase the COMIC off.)*

BLACKOUT

*D*rag acts were more common in English music halls than in Burlesque. But a number of American comics, notably Tony Hart and Joe Yule, Mickey Rooney's father, specialized in playing silly harridans.

Clearly, there is good reason occasionally to put a comedian into a dress. Many jokes have a female point of view. But it would be out of character for an elegant prima donna to speak them. A man in drag can say things with impunity that would be resented from a real woman.

With David Campbell, I adapted "Nursemaids" from a number of classic Burlesque scenes and from the wonderful act of an English comedian, Rex Jameson, who billed himself as Mrs. Shufflewick. He was not a camp artist in glamorous drag like Danny La Rue or a social satirist with a gay sensibility like Charles Ludlum. Mrs. Shufflewick was a working-class washerwoman with a Rabelaisian sense of humor, almost like Petunia in the sketch.

```
○○○○○○○○○○○○○○○○○○○○○○○○○○
○                                            ○
○                                            ○
○        DRIVING BABY BUGGY                  ○
○         ("Nursemaids")                     ○
○                                            ○
○                                            ○
○○○○○○○○○○○○○○○○○○○○○○○○○○
```

Musical play-on. The curtains part to reveal a drop depicting Battery Park. A park bench is C. PRUDENCE (3RD COMIC) enters in a nursemaid's dress, pushing a baby carriage and yelling at the unseen, squalling baby.

PRUDENCE Now, Cecil, take that out of your mouth. *(SHE takes a pacifier from the baby's mouth. The baby cries.)* And stop playing with that rattle. *(swipes at the baby with her purse)* I don't care how wet you are, you nasty little thing. You can lie there and soak for all I care! *(A handsome POLICEMAN strolls by. SHE primps and suddenly gets very sweet with the baby.)* Gootchy, gootchy, goo! What's the matter, my little lambkins? Ozzums gottums tootsums wootsums wet? Nursie-wursie's here to put it all right. *(The POLICEMAN exits.)* Rotten little kid!

(SHE swipes at the baby again, crosses to the bench and parks her carriage to the R. of it. SHE sits, takes a flask from her purse and has a nip. A second carriage comes flying out of the wings and almost goes into the orchestra pit. Hot in pursuit is PATIENCE [2ND COMIC] in a neat dress. SHE catches the runaway carriage just in time.)

PATIENCE Little beggar almost got away from me. *(to baby)* You do that again, you little thumb sucker, and I'll let you float to Staten Island. *(SHE backs her carriage to L. of bench.)*

PRUDENCE Where's Petunia?

PATIENCE She's right behind me. She's huffing and puffing these days. She's gotten a little wide in the beam. *(PATIENCE sits next to PRUDENCE.)*

PRUDENCE *(handing flask to PATIENCE)* Well, at least she's kept her figure.

PATIENCE *(taking flask)* Kept it! She's doubled it! *(PATIENCE sips. Enter PETUNIA [1ST COMIC] in elaborate drag, pushing a third carriage. SHE is exhausted.)*

PETUNIA Hello, girls.

PRUDENCE Hello, Petunia. You look a little tuckered out.

PETUNIA (*parking carriage to the L. of PATIENCE's*) This has got to be the fattest baby on Manhattan Island. Takes all my strength just to push the little monster. (*SHE crosses to bench and sits with the other TWO.*)

PATIENCE Well, rest a spell and have a nip. (*PATIENCE passes the flask to PETUNIA. The baby in R. carriage cries. ALL THREE lean and look into the carriage.*) Oh, that is a pitiful looking child!

PRUDENCE It's a matter of breeding. Money can't buy looks.

PETUNIA There ain't nothing in the world homelier than a plain Park Avenue baby. (*The baby in one of the L. carriages cries. ALL lean L. and look at it.*)

PATIENCE Look at my Rodney. He's got one brown eye and one blue one.

PETUNIA One from each of his fathers, I expect.

PRUDENCE These rich folk ain't got no morals at all.

ALL (*return to upright position*) Mmmmmmm.

PATIENCE (*to change the subject, stands to show off her dress*) How do you like my uniform? I got it for my thirtieth birthday.

PETUNIA Wore well, didn't it?

PATIENCE Now, just wait a second, Miss Petunia. Everybody says I have the skin of a seventeen-year old girl. (*SHE sits again.*)

PETUNIA Well, you need to give it back. You're getting it wrinkled. (*SHE passes the flask to PATIENCE.*)

PATIENCE Look who's talking. You ain't no spring lamb yourself.

PETUNIA I ain't lost it yet, girls. I ain't lost it yet.

PATIENCE & PRUDENCE (*as PRUDENCE takes the flask*) Hah! (*PRUDENCE sips.*)

PETUNIA (*highly offended*) They still come running! I was down at the Blue Moon Cafe, and I ran into that handsome night watchman. You know the one I mean—the one who always shines his lantern up my alley.

PATIENCE No!

PETUNIA Yes! We had a few gins together without a word passing

141

between us. Then, he flashes a roll of greenbacks and peels one off. "Come on back to my place," he said, "and this can be yours."

PATIENCE (*interested in spite of herself*) Why, that dirty thing! What did you do?

PETUNIA I stayed cool, calm and collected.

PATIENCE You always were man-crazy, Petunia. Not me, I'm through with the whole beastly bunch. I'm going to become a nun.

PRUDENCE Honey, you're already a nun. You ain't had none, you ain't got none, and you ain't never going to get none.

PATIENCE (*taking the flask*) I resent that, Prudence. I've had plenty of suitors in my time.

PETUNIA Yeah. Too bad your time is up.

PATIENCE I can't help it if I have high standards.

PETUNIA Do tell.

PRUDENCE Marriage would be all right if you could do it alone.

PETUNIA Yeah, but a man always gets mixed up in it.

(*There is an arpeggio from the ORCHESTRA, as PATIENCE begins to sing.*)

CHOOSING A HUSBAND'S A DELICATE THING

Lyrics by Ralph Allen &   Music by Michael Valenti
David Campbell

PETUNIA I LOOKED FOR PERFECTION AND WOULD NOT TAKE LESS.
YES, TOM WAS TOO TIDY, AND MIKE WAS A MESS.
CHUCK CHEWED TOBACCO, AND TO MY DISTRESS
I KEPT CATCHING DAN IN MY CORSET AND DRESS.
(*Spoken*)
Choosing a husband's a delicate thing.

(*SHE takes a sip from the flask and hands it to PRUDENCE.*)

PRUDENCE & PETUNIA (*spoken*) Ain't it the truth!

ALL THREE (*singing*) OHHHHHHH...(*a little tipsy, THEY rush to their respective carriages.*)

PATIENCE CHOOSING A HUSBAND'S A DELICATE THING!

ALL THREE (*swinging their carriages to and fro in time to the music*) OH, YES! IT'S A DELICATE THING!

SOON WE'LL BE OVER LIFE'S SEASON OF SPRING!
CHOOSING A HUSBAND'S A DELICATE, DELICATE THING!

(THEY dance with the baby carriages and are clearly getting drunk. THEY come to a stop. The music continues under the dialogue.)

PRUDENCE *(waving the flask)* That's our fate, girls; always a nursemaid, never to nurse.

PETUNIA You said it, sister!

PRUDENCE I never wanted to be a wife.

PATIENCE Is that so?

PRUDENCE I wanted to be a widow. But I put all my eggs in one basket.

PETUNIA I remember. You took up with Henry McNabb, that old man. I say, that mummy who ran the pawn shop on 22nd Street.

PATIENCE *(sniffing)* Lived in sin with him.

PRUDENCE It was a sin, all right. When I think of the time I wasted feeding him pills and rubbing camphor all over his joints.

PETUNIA The things you had to put up with.

PRUDENCE Girls, it was terrible. Every night I felt old age creeping up on me.

PATIENCE You had it soft.

PRUDENCE That's true, too. It was the same old thing, weak in, weak out.

(THEY ALL sing, skipping with their carriages, again in time to the music.)

ALL OHHHHHHH....
CHOOSING A HUSBAND'S A DELICATE THING!
YOU BET! IT'S A DELICATE THING!
TO MORE THAN ONE BASKET YOUR EGGS YOU SHOULD
  BRING!
CHOOSING A HUSBAND'S A DELICATE, DELICATE THING!

(There is another dance interlude as the GIRLS, much drunker now, push the carriages around the stage.)

PATIENCE *(when THEY have come to an unsteady halt)* No man's worth all that grief!

PETUNIA You girls should spread yourselves around a little more.

PATIENCE A lot of good it did you.

PRUDENCE I don't see a ring on *your* finger.

PETUNIA I know, girls; I know. But it wasn't my fault. Beauty's a burden.

PRUDENCE & PATIENCE *(sighing)* How true! How true!
(PATIENCE passes the flask from PRUDENCE to PETUNIA.)

PETUNIA My good looks and my good nature did me in.

PRUDENCE *(sympathetically)* Sugar, you have been on more laps than a napkin.

(Three sheets to the wind now. THEY ALL cross to the carriages and sing. As THEY start the chorus, THEY fling the carriages back and forth to one another.)

ALL THREE *(raucously)* OHHHHHHH...
CHOOSING A HUSBAND'S A DELICATE THING!
BET YOUR ASS IT'S A DELICATE THING!
WE ALWAYS QUIVER WHEN WEDDING BELLS RING! RING,
RING, RING!
CHOOSING A HUSBAND'S A DELICATE, DELICATE THING!

(ALL three carriages, careening, head for the orchestra pit and are caught just in time. The GIRLS screech to a halt, bonnets askew, shirt-waists disarranged. All of the babies are squalling at the top of their lungs.)

PRUDENCE That woke the little droolers up.

PATIENCE *(looking at the babies with some dismay)* Say, is that my Rodney? Or is that your Cecil?

PRUDENCE Damned if I know.

PETUNIA What difference does it make, girls? They all look alike, anyway.

(THEY exit, chattering away as the babies yell.)

BLACKOUT

"The Knife Thrower" is a version of an old Burlesque scene called "The Sharpshooter." Ernest Flatt, the director of *Sugar Babies*, argued that machetes were more interesting visually than bullets, and, of course, he was right.

This version of the sketch was written with Eddie Bracken in mind. Mickey Rooney has to be an agitator, the center of energy in a scene. Bracken, on the other hand, has specialized for years in playing comic victims. (Remember "The Miracle of Morgan's Creek.") When Eddie was cast first in a road company of *Sugar Babies*, then in the Australian tour, we all learned an important lesson. Low comedy has to be tailored to the style and personality of the principal comic.

Various prima donnas—Carol Channing and Jane Summerhays among them—have played the myopic Madam Vivosectovitch. I have printed the knife-thrower's dialect in plain English. But often the actress used a generic Balkan accent with W's for V's, etc.

THE WORLD'S GREATEST KNIFE-THROWER

ANNOUNCER *(enters at L. proscenium)* Ladies and gentlemen, please welcome to the Gaiety Theatre—that lynx-eyed mistress of the steel blade—the world's greatest knife-thrower, Madam Vivesectovitch.

(Fanfare. The PRIMA DONNA as the KNIFE-THROWER appears C. through the pink curtain. SHE has a whip in her belt. The curtains part to reveal at R. proscenium a knifeboard with the silhouette of a man painted on it. A table L., on which some knives are placed.)

KNIFE-THROWER Thank you, ladies and gentlemen, I need an assistant from the audience. Anyone who assists me receives a crisp new hundred-dollar bill. Oh, there's a young man that needs some money. Good, sir. Come right up here onto the stage. *(A sad-eyed COMIC climbs to the stage from the auditorium.)* Let's give this accommodating man a great big hand. *(applause, perhaps)* Thank you for coming forward.

COMIC Glad to help. Where's my hundred dollars?

KNIFE-THROWER *(taking a bill from her pocket and tearing it)* You get half now...*(gives him half)*...and half when the trick is over. *(puts other half in her pocket)*

COMIC That seems fair. *(KNIFE-THROWER guides COMIC to board. SHE takes a cigarette from her pocket.)*

KNIFE-THROWER Now, sir, just stand over there...*(COMIC does so.)* ...and put the cigarette in your mouth.

COMIC Thank you very much, but I don't smoke.

KNIFE-THROWER No, you don't understand. I'm going to stand over there and throw a knife at that cigarette.

COMIC You're going to what?

KNIFE-THROWER I'm going to cut that cigarette in half with my knife.

I used to have a regular assistant...

COMIC Oh, no, you're not. *(SHE cracks the whip.)*

KNIFE-THROWER Back against the board. Back! *(HE cowers against the board. SHE sharpens a knife.)* That's better. I used to have a regular assistant when I did this act before.

COMIC Oh, you did?

KNIFE-THROWER Yes, he was a little fellow about your size. I called him little Sylvester.

COMIC That's a nice name.

KNIFE-THROWER But he's no longer with me. Now for my first trick.

COMIC What happened to little Sylvester?

KNIFE-THROWER Oh, well. You know how it is. Ladies and gentlemen, for my first display of skill...

COMIC *(more firmly)* I don't know how it is. What happened to little Sylvester?

KNIFE-THROWER Well, if you must know, one night between shows, I had an argument with that Bulgarian son of a gypsy who calls himself my husband, and I was a little nervous. I was getting ready to throw a knife at little Sylvester's cigarette, and I missed the cigarette. The press was very unkind. I didn't miss by much. What's a few inches more or less after all these years?

COMIC *(starts to go)* So long. I'll see you later.

KNIFE-THROWER No, come back. You see, that night my hand was shaking. My hand doesn't shake any more. *(her hand is shaking)*

COMIC It doesn't shake any less, either.

KNIFE-THROWER Remember the hundred dollars.

COMIC It's a good thing for you that I'm greedy. *(goes to board)*

KNIFE-THROWER Are you ready?

COMIC Yes.

KNIFE-THROWER Are you at the board?

COMIC Yes, I'm against the...You can't see the board? You're going to throw a knife at that board, and you can't see it?

KNIFE-THROWER I'm not throwing at the board. I'm throwing at the cigarette.

COMIC *(laughs)* That's right. *(to AUDIENCE)* The board's got nothing to do with it.

KNIFE-THROWER Are you ready?

COMIC Yes.

KNIFE-THROWER Are you against the board?

COMIC Yes.

KNIFE-THROWER Is the cigarette in your mouth?

COMIC Yes, it's in my...*(HE stops short.)* You can't see the cigarette? You're going to throw a knife at the cigarette, and you can't see it?

KNIFE-THROWER *(myopically)* Keep talking. I'll find you. Are you ready?

COMIC Yeah.

KNIFE-THROWER Here we go. One...two...Wait! Wait!

COMIC What now?

KNIFE-THROWER I've got a better idea. Turn and face me. *(COMIC faces her, his cigarette dangling from his mouth.)* Ladies and gentlemen, tonight I'm going to perform the most difficult test ever attempted by a knife-thrower. I'm going to throw and split that cigarette right down the middle.

COMIC Hey...that is a terrific trick. She's going to split that cigarette down the middle...*(sudden realization)*...and split my head right with it. I'm going home. I forgot something.

KNIFE-THROWER What did you forget?

COMIC I forgot to stay there.

KNIFE-THROWER No, come back. You're right. I'll play it safe.

COMIC *(stopping)* You will?

KNIFE-THROWER Sure. I'll do it exactly as I did it with little Sylvester.

COMIC Well, that's better.

KNIFE-THROWER Ready? *(a fanfare)* One...two...three. (SHE throws first knife which lands near the COMIC's ankle.) Ooops. Missed. (SHE throws a second knife which just misses his shoulder.) Getting closer. (The third knife misses the board, and we hear a scream offstage. A pause) Completely missed the board. (A fourth knife whizzes past the COMIC's *ear.)* That's better. *(The last knife catches the board right between the COMIC's legs. HE is paralyzed with fear.)* Ladies and gentlemen, there stands a brave man. He didn't even move.

COMIC That's what you think.

BLACKOUT

He didn't even move.

"The Knife-Thrower," like "The Egg in the Hat," is a presentational scene. By that I mean it takes place in the theatre, not in a restaurant or schoolroom or a court. The fiction is that a real act, a planned part of the show is somehow going awry.

The most elaborate presentational scenes are crammed with interruption jokes. The premise is time-honored not only in Burlesque, but in Vaudeville and English Music Hall as well.

A pretentious artist is performing an ostensibly serious act—reciting poetry, playing a musical instrument, or more usually, singing operatic arias. Meanwhile, the comics interrupt her (or him) with outrageous questions and impertinent gags. Finally, they drive her mad. Professor Lamberti's famous vaudeville turn was a sketch of this sort, and the Broadway entertainments of Olsen and Johnson carried the device to its logical extreme.

In *Sugar Babies*, "Madame Gazaza," our big second-act interruption scene, was adapted from two well-known Burlesque sketches "The Hammer Scene" and "Crazy House." Ann Miller played a desperate opera singer who was subjected to scandalous indignities and who finally collapsed under the pressure. Everyone knew that Ann was a wonderful dancer and singer, but Madame Gazaza proved that she was also a brilliant sketch comedian.

PRESENTING MADAME GAZAZA
("Hammer Scene" & "Crazy House")

Enter STRAIGHT in tuxedo. He stands in front of traveler.

STRAIGHT And now, ladies and gentlemen, the management would like to introduce this week's feature attraction...

(CANDY BUTCHER* appears in the aisle with his tray around his neck. HE has some balloons for sale.)

CANDY BUTCHER Rubber balloons, souvenirs, peanuts, candy, rubber balloons.

STRAIGHT Wait a minute, pal, you can't sell your balloons here. There's a show going on.

CANDY BUTCHER Gee, I'm sorry. You see, I haven't been myself lately. I just got married, and I haven't been getting any sleep.

STRAIGHT Yeah, and that reminds me, _____, don't forget to pull the shade down when you're in bed with your wife.

CANDY BUTCHER What are you talking about?

STRAIGHT I drove past your house last night. Your shade was up, and I saw you making love to your wife.

CANDY BUTCHER Ha! The joke's on you. I wasn't home last night. *(HE does a delayed take, then exits up the aisle shouting, "Rubber balloons! Rubber balloons!")*

STRAIGHT Excuse the interruption, ladies and gentlemen. The Gaiety Theatre is no ordinary palace of vulgar entertainment. Our audiences know class when they see it. So let's give a typical Gaiety welcome to that queen of the mezzo-sopranos, Madame Alla Gazaza.

(Fanfare. STRAIGHT exits as curtain parts to reveal PRIMA DONNA as MADAME GAZAZA in evening gown. SHE is flanked by potted

---

*A "butcher" in show business was a saleman.

plants. S.L. is a piano. An ACCOMPANIST in tails plays an arpeggio. MADAME GAZAZA begins singing an aria. Enter 1ST COMIC in the middle of the audience. HE is dressed in overalls. HE starts to hammer. SHE continues to sing for a few bars, then stops angrily.)

GAZAZA What are you doing?

1ST COMIC I'm hammering.

GAZAZA But I'm singing.

1ST COMIC Well, go ahead, sweetheart, you're not bothering me.

GAZAZA What's the big idea?

1ST COMIC Well, the manager told me to make some repairs. I'm fixing seats. *(to a LADY in the audience)* Would you like to have your seat fixed?

GAZAZA Now, listen, little man. If you don't behave, I'm going to ask the manager to take you out.

1ST COMIC I don't go out with managers.

GAZAZA How dare you insult the great Gazaza. I have sung before the crowned heads of Europe.

1ST COMIC *(removing hat to show bald spot)* And the bald heads of [LOCAL]. *(1ST COMIC may find some occasions for ad lib comment here. If there is a bald man seated near him, HE might compare heads or make some appropriate comment like, "Pardon me, sir, I thought you were sitting upside down.")*

GAZAZA What effrontery, young man! I have one of the most expensive voices in the world. I spent fifty thousand dollars to train this voice.

1ST COMIC What did you do with the money? *(HE mounts the stage.)* Fifty thousand dollars? You ought to meet my brother.

GAZAZA Is he a voice teacher?

1ST COMIC No, he's a lawyer. He'll help you get your money back. *(HE exits L., as SHE calls off R.)*

GAZAZA Mr. _____. Mr. _____.

STRAIGHT *(enters R.)* What is it now, Madame Gazaza?

GAZAZA There's a little man out here, and he keeps insulting me.

STRAIGHT What little man? *(apologetically)* Opera singers are very eccentric.

GAZAZA I am not eccentric.

STRAIGHT Compose yourself, Madame Gazaza. The show must go on.

GAZAZA Yes, of course. Please excuse the interruptions, ladies and gentlemen. I will now try to sing a different tune. Maestro. (*SHE starts singing.*)

2ND COMIC (*enters R. with a mournful expression on his face*) Oh, why did he die? Why did he die?

GAZAZA (*stops singing*) Why did who die?

2ND COMIC My wife's first husband. Why did he die? (*exits L. GAZAZA begins singing again. 1ST COMIC enters L. and crosses the stage in tight circles, grunting and making karate chops.*)

GAZAZA Who are you?

1ST COMIC I'm a vicious circle. (*1ST COMIC exits R. as CHARACTER MAN enters R., looking into a large hand mirror.*)

CHARACTER It can't be. It can't be. Who's that? (*HE puts mirror up to GAZAZA's face.*)

GAZAZA Me.

CHARACTER Thank God, I thought it was me. (*exit L. GAZAZA is bewildered. SHE sings a note or two, but without much confidence. Enter 2ND COMIC L.*)

2ND COMIC Hey, how do you kiss the rear end of a duck without getting feathers in your mouth?

GAZAZA I don't know.

2ND COMIC (*pantomimes blowing, then kissing*) But you got to be fast. (*exit R. GAZAZA sings briefly as JUVENILE enters R., skipping rope.*)

GAZAZA What are you doing?

JUVENILE I'm following doctor's orders.

GAZAZA Doctor's orders?

JUVENILE Yes, he told me to take some pills three days running, then skip a day. This is my day to skip. (*HE skips off R. GAZAZA seems about to sing, when 2ND COMIC enters R. with a mouthful of feathers.*)

2ND COMIC (*to AUDIENCE*) I wasn't fast enough. (*HE exits L. as CHARACTER MAN enters R.*)

CHARACTER (*trying to get GAZAZA's attention*) Madame. Madame. What's the difference between mashed potatoes and pea soup?

GAZAZA I don't know.

CHARACTER Anyone can mash potatoes. *(HE exits L. as GAZAZA makes one last effort to sing. 1ST COMIC enters moaning.)*

1ST COMIC Why did I do it? Why did I do it?

GAZAZA Do what?

1ST COMIC I sold my wife for a bottle of whiskey, and now I want her back.

GAZAZA Do you miss her?

1ST COMIC No, but I'm thirsty again. *(HE remains on as SOUBRETTE enters R. SHE crosses the stage crying and bumping.)*

SOUBRETTE My husband is dead, dead, dead. *(bumps)* My husband is dead, dead, dead. *(bumps. SHE has reached 1ST COMIC.)* My husband is dead, dead, dead...DEAD! *(exits L.)*

1ST COMIC *(calling off after her)* Your husband ain't dead. He's hiding. *(HE exits R. as CANDY BUTCHER appears in the R. aisle.)* On second thought, maybe you bumped him off.

CANDY BUTCHER Souvenirs. Candy. Rubber balloons. Get your rubber balloons.

GAZAZA *(calling R.)* Mr. _____. Mr. _____.

STRAIGHT *(entering R.)* What's the matter now?

GAZAZA I'm nearing the end of my endurance. Why is that man selling balloons?

STRAIGHT What's the matter with you, pal? I told you before you can't sell balloons while the show...By the way, do you sell refreshments, too?

CANDY BUTCHER Sure.

STRAIGHT Do you have popcorn balls?

CANDY BUTCHER No, rheumatism makes me walk this way. *(HE exits angrily up the aisle, hollering, "Rubber balloons.")*

STRAIGHT *(very apologetically)* Continue singing, Madame Gazaza. You won't have any further trouble. *(HE exits R.)*

GAZAZA All right. Ladies and gentlemen, I have a request. But I'm gonna sing anyway. I will now sing "ONE FINE DAY" by Madame Butterfly. *(to ACCOMPANIST, sharply)* Hit it, Knuckles. *(SHE sings.)*

1ST COMIC *(enter L. with a large light bulb)* Twenty years of my life I've devoted to this invention. My family has gone without food and shelter. But now, I'll be rich; I'll be the toast of the scientific world.

Finally, it's perfected. The world will know me at last. *(talking into bulb as if it were a telephone)* Hello. Hello. *(1ST COMIC exits R. as JUVENILE and CHARACTER MAN enter R., running and quarreling.)*

JUVENILE Take it back.

CHARACTER I won't.

JUVENILE You will.

CHARACTER I won't. *(The JUVENILE shoots the CHARACTER MAN. The LATTER starts to fall. The JUVENILE runs quickly behind the CHARACTER MAN and catches him, dragging him L.)*

GAZAZA *(almost hysterical)* Mr. _____, he's killed him! I can't stand it anymore.!

STRAIGHT *(enters, followed by a GORILLA on roller skates, carrying a bouquet)* Here's a fan of yours, Madame Gazaza. *(GORILLA skates toward her and presents her with the bouquet. GAZAZA doesn't see the GORILLA until after SHE accepts the flowers.)*

GAZAZA Oh, thank you. *(SHE sees the GORILLA, screams and faints. The STRAIGHT MAN catches her, as the TWO COMICS enter, one from each side, to aid the STRAIGHT.)*

STRAIGHT Rub her neck. *(TWO COMICS echo it.)* Rub her arms. *(TWO COMICS echo it.)* Rub her shoulder. *(TWO COMICS echo it. Enter CANDY BUTCHER L. with balloons.)*

CANDY BUTCHER Rubber balloons...rubber balloons...

BLACKOUT

Like "Madame Gazaza," "The Pancake" is an interruption scene, but on a much more modest scale. I include it here as a memorial to Billy Foster, of the great Columbia team of Harcourt and Foster. Billy performed this scene from 1912 when he made his debut in Burlesque until 1965 when he was almost ninety. I only saw him near the end of his career, but even as an octogenarian he had a wry impish wit that was completely captivating.

THE PANCAKE

In front of Salvation Army headquarters. STRAIGHT beating bass drum, TWO GIRLS playing tambourines and singing with STRAIGHT.

STRAIGHT I'LL SAVE YOU; I'LL SAVE YOU.
   OH, COME TO ME, AND I'LL SAVE YOU.
Oh, brothers and sisters, let me tell you how the Good Book saved my life in the last war. *(COMIC enters during this speech.)*

COMIC Hi, _____. How's your mother?

STRAIGHT My mother's all right. Don't interrupt me. Oh, brothers and sisters, let me tell you...

COMIC I really miss your mother. She's a fine cook.

STRAIGHT Yes, she's an excellent cook. But don't you see I'm talking here. I'm saving sinners.

COMIC Your mother can sure make pancakes.

STRAIGHT Yes, she makes good pancakes.

COMIC Yes, good and hard.

STRAIGHT Drop the pancakes.

COMIC If I dropped them, they'd knock a hole in the floor.

STRAIGHT *(walking away disgustedly)* Well, don't mind me. There's my audience out there. Give them plenty of pancakes.

COMIC If I did they'd all drop dead. *(sees that STRAIGHT is mad)* I'm sorry, _____. Go back to saving sinners. I won't say anything more about pancakes.

STRAIGHT Brothers and sisters, let me tell you how the Good Book saved my life during the war. My mother said to me when I enlisted in the 17th Dragoons, "Son, I want you to carry this prayer book next to your heart." It was in the winter of '18. We were trying to reach the Carcassonne Ridge. The boy carrying the Star Spangled Banner fell dead in his tracks, the victim of a German bullet. The captain of my company cried, "Who will save the Star Spangled Banner?" I jumped up.

COMIC *(to AUDIENCE)* Somebody goosed him.

STRAIGHT *(ignoring him)* I grabbed the flag and planted it on top of the ridge. But as I did, a machine gun bullet hit me here. *(HE points to his heart.)*

COMIC And killed you?

STRAIGHT No, it hit the prayer book, the one my mother gave me. That prayer book saved my life. Now, brothers and sisters...

COMIC What a coincidence!

STRAIGHT What did you say?

COMIC I was a hero, too.

STRAIGHT Is that so?

COMIC It was in the winter of '22.

STRAIGHT There was no war in '22.

COMIC It's easy to see you don't know Newark. The Star Spangled Banana fell to the ground. All around me were codfish balls and snowballs.

STRAIGHT How come?

COMIC It was Friday in the dead of winter.

STRAIGHT What happened?

COMIC My captain said, "Who is brave enough to save the stars and strips?"

STRAIGHT You mean the stars and stripes.

COMIC That's right. I jumped up, grabbed the flag and stuck it in a hedge. And as I did a machine gun bullet caught me here.

STRAIGHT And a prayer book saved you.

COMIC Not a prayer book.

STRAIGHT What was it then?

COMIC One of your mother's pancakes.

BLACKOUT

Lowbrow and highbrow tastes tend to coincide. As one might expect, therefore, Burlesque had a devoted following among intellectuals. Only middlebrows, like Mayor Laguardia, disapproved of it. Oliver Wendell Holmes used to escape the pressures of the Supreme Court by making weekly visits to the Washington Gaiety at 9th and E Streets. And Edmund Wilson was a devoted admirer of the Minsky shows. Other habitués included Hart Crane, Reginald Marsh, E. E. Cummings and H. L. Mencken.

However, the great majority of Burlesque patrons were not well-educated. Many of them were immigrants who knew only a smattering of English, and the native-born in the audience were not sophisticated readers.

As a result, you could not expect to find literary satire at the Gaiety or any scenes that required a detailed knowledge of history. In fact, the only historical figures who regularly found their way into the skits were Adam and Eve, or Julius Squeezer and Cleopotroast.

Edmund Wilson has left us an enthusiastic account of Cleopotroast's affair with Tony the Bootblack as it was dramatized at Minsky's. My own version of the scene not only draws on the sketch that Wilson describes, but on another famous but non-historical scene, "The Gun Ain't Loaded."

The curtain parts and the lights come up to reveal CLEOPOTROAST's barge. CLEOPOTROAST is on a purple couch, surrounded by GIRLS. EUNUCH SLAVES (3RD and 4TH COMICS) are fanning her with giant feather fans on long poles. The setting is like a tent barge on the Nile. It is lavish, but still "Burlesque." CLEOPOTROAST's SERVANT GIRLS, i.e., the CHORUS, perform an Egyptian dance. Along with the sound of finger cymbals and drums, the GIRLS are wailing in an Eastern way, and the music is loud. Over the din we hear CLEOPOTROAST doing her own wailing, but hers is from an obvious hangover. Eventually SHE can't stand it any longer and by banging a giant cymbal, which does nothing for her hangover, SHE stops the proceedings.

CLEOPOTROAST Enough, slaves, enough. I'm weary. Begone! Begone! *(THEY start to exit.)* Not thee, Charmian. *(CHARMIAN remains as OTHERS depart.)* Hast seen my asp today?

CHARMIAN Nay, not since your morning bath.

CLEOPOTROAST Oh, dear. *(A bugle sounds. Enter EUNUCH in haste.)*

EUNUCH Oh, Cleopotroast. A handsome Roman awaits without.

CLEOPOTROAST Without what?

EUNUCH Without food and clothing.

CLEOPOTROAST Well, feed him and send him in. *(EUNUCH exits.)* Perhaps he brings us news about the palace parley. Even now as we languish on this barge, brave Antony and cold Octavius Squeezer are meeting. They're searching jointly for a lasting peace.

CHARMIAN I could use a piece myself, fair queen. *(enter 1ST COMIC as LASCIVIUS, in a short skirt with no shirt)*

LASCIVIUS Oh, noble queen, I lay my Roman heart at your Egyptian feet.

I am Lascivius, a humble messenger.

CLEOPOTROAST Who art thou?

LASCIVIUS I am Lascivius, a humble messenger. The peace is broken off.

CLEOPOTROAST Oh, no, what happened?

LASCIVIUS Squeezer made demands. He said Antony must mend his ways.

CLEOPOTROAST What ways?

LASCIVIUS To share the throne, he must give up his picnics, his parties and his balls. He tried, great queen—gave up his picnics...

CLEOPOTROAST Yes?

LASCIVIUS Gave up his parties...

CLEOPOTROAST Yes?

LASCIVIUS But where would he be without his b...

CLEOPOTROAST Yes, Lascivius, I get thy drift.

LASCIVIUS Ah, queen, I am sandal-sore. Canst put me up?

CLEOPOTROAST The barge is booked.

CHARMIAN Yon purple couch is free. He could sleep there.

CLEOPOTROAST Thou seemst a bit eager, wench. And yet, 'tis not a bad idea. *(to LASCIVIUS)* Thou mayest rest upon that purple pallet. But mark me well, Lascivius...*(pointing to R. doorway)*...that door leads to the chamber where I sleep, and nought but Tony may darken it. *(pointing to L. doorway)* And over there dwells Charmian; she is betrothed to Enobarbus. And if thy foot approach her portal, thou shalt surely die.

LASCIVIUS Die? How?

CLEOPOTROAST My sacred asp will do thee in. It is quick to bite.

LASCIVIUS Don't tell me your asp has teeth?

CHARMIAN She means her snake, Lascivius—the poison serpent that got loose this morning.

LASCIVIUS Oh, that asp. That's different. Got lost, did it? *(attempting to go)* Well, toodles, girls. I'll see you later.

CLEOPOTROAST Nay, my asp would never crawl into thy purple couch. Thou hast no need to fear...provided that thy feet stay put and *never* touch the floor.

LASCIVIUS *(reassured)* Oh, don't worry about me. I'm tuckered out and fain would hit the hay.

CLEOPOTROAST We take no chances here. Bring me the mating musk. *(CHARMIAN fetches a stone pot.)*

LASCIVIUS The what?

CLEOPOTROAST The mating musk. It has a scent that doth attract the rampant asp and sends him straight into a frenzy. Pour it, wench, upon the Roman's feet; then go. *(CHARMIAN does so. LASCIVIUS quickly hops into the bed and covers his feet with pillows.)*

CHARMIAN *(flirting; a little bump on her exit)* Goodnight, Lascivius. If thou needst anything, just call.

LASCIVIUS If anything comes up during the night, I will contact thee. *(SHE exits. CLEOPOTROAST is at her door.)*

CLEOPOTROAST *(exiting)* Go to sleep now, and don't forget my asp.

LASCIVIUS Don't worry, queen. I'll think about it all night long. Goodnight. *(HE makes himself comfortable, goes to sleep as CHARMIAN enters and tiptoes over to the bed.)*

CHARMIAN Psssst.

LASCIVIUS *(looking under bed, not seeing CHARMIAN)* Ye gods! The asp!

CHARMIAN Psssst.

LASCIVIUS 'Tis a hissing asp. It hisses, hits you, then you're gone.

CHARMIAN Psssst.

LASCIVIUS *(seeing her)* Oh, hello, Charmian. I thought thou wert in bed.

CHARMIAN *(beckoning)* Come, little Roman, come.

LASCIVIUS That's a nice thought, maid, and by Jupiter, I hate to turn thee down. In fact, it is a first for me. And yet, I must say nay.

CHARMIAN Why?

LASCIVIUS The asp is loose.

CHARMIAN The asp isn't loose. 'Tis but a garter snake.

LASCIVIUS A garter snake?

CHARMIAN Come, little Roman, come. *(CHARMIAN exits L.)*

LASCIVIUS Well, if 'tis but a garter snake...*(A loud snore comes from CLEOPOTROAST's chamber.)* Ah! Cleopotroast snores within. I'll slip into the maid's chamber and right back out before the queen suspects.

> *(HE exits L. as CLEOPOTROAST enters R., approaching the couch and looking for him.)*

CLEOPOTROAST Lascivius? Lascivius? Wherefore art thou, Lascivius? Perhaps he strolleth on the poop deck. But he'll be back. And so will I. And so will I. *(SHE exits R. LASCIVIUS enters, backing onstage while talking to the offstage CHARMIAN.)*

LASCIVIUS I thank thee, girl. I thank thee very much. *(goes to couch and lies on it)* But now my eyelids droop. 'Tis time to say goodnight.

CLEOPOTROAST *(peeks on from R.)* Psssst.

LASCIVIUS *(eyes closed)* Ah, Charmian. Hast thou not had enough? Besides, if Cleopotroast catches us, she'll feed me to the crocodiles.

CLEOPOTROAST Psssst.

LASCIVIUS *(Opening eyes and seeing her, HE is upset.)* Oh, Cleopotroast! There you are. I'm sorry if I woke thee up. I talketh in my sleep, and what I talk about has nought to do with what I say...

CLEOPOTROAST Come on in.

LASCIVIUS Oh, no. The royal asp is loose.

CLEOPOTROAST The asp isn't loose. I spoofeth you.

LASCIVIUS You spoofeth? But the mating musk?

Pssst.

But he'll be back. And so will I. And so will I!

CLEOPOTROAST *(exiting seductively)* Nothing but a cheap cologne. Come on in.

LASCIVIUS *(at door to AUDIENCE)* Tarry, friends. I shan't take long. I never do. *(HE exits R., almost immediately CHARMIAN enters.)*

CHARMIAN Oh, Lascivius? Lascivius? *(not finding him)* I wonder where that little Roman's gone. Ah, perhaps he's airing out his sandals. But he'll be back. And so will I. *(at door with increasing fervor)* And so will I!

LASCIVIUS *(calling off to CLEOPOTROAST)* Enough, fair queen, enough. 'Tis very gracious, but that's my limit. In fact, I've gone one over it already. In sooth, I'm set for the next year. Verily, 'tis a good thing, but run it not into the ground. *(As HE closes his eyes, CHARMIAN enters.)*

CHARMIAN Psssst.

LASCIVIUS Not you again.

CHARMIAN Psssst.

LASCIVIUS Doth no one sleep in Egypt?

CHARMIAN Come, little Roman, come.

LASCIVIUS *(feebly)* The asp is loose.

CHARMIAN It isn't loose.

LASCIVIUS Well, I wish it was.

CHARMIAN *(at door)* Come on in.

LASCIVIUS I need some of Squeezer's virility pills. They're very strong. Thou hast to swallow them fast. Otherwise, thou wilt get a stiff neck. *(HE exits, and CLEOPOTROAST enters almost immediately.)*

CLEOPOTROAST Lascivius! Lascivius! Where is my little Roman candle? Oh, he's gone again! He's a nervous little fellow, but he'll be back. And so will I! And so will I!

(SHE exits as LASCIVIUS appears walking on his hands. His leg is apparently being held by CHARMIAN offstage.)

LASCIVIUS *(a wreck now)* Oh, maid, release that leg. Desist, I say! Lock up? Lock up! Barbarians are coming! They rape and pillage! And if they aren't coming, I'll send for them. *(HE is in bed, all but his right leg, which is resting like a dead weight on the floor. HE lifts the leg onto*

Well, I wish it was!

167

The asp is in my grasp!

the couch, using both hands.) Come on, don't you die on me, too. Goodnight! *(HE is prostrate with exhaustion. CLEOPOTROAST enters.)*

CLEOPOTROAST *(imperiously)* Up, Lascivius. Up, I say! The queen commands your presence.

LASCIVIUS Command away, oh, queen. I can't get up. It may be several months before I'm up again. *(CLEOPOTROAST grabs him by the neck and starts dragging him off.)*

CLEOPOTROAST Come, we waste words.

LASCIVIUS *(weakly)* An asp...an asp...my kingdom for an asp. *(THEY exit as CHARMIAN enters. SHE whistles and ALL the rest of the EGYPTIAN GIRLS enter giggling.)*

CHARMIAN Lascivius. Lascivius. Art thou hiding again, thou little Roman rascal? Don't worry, girls, he can't be far. *(a trumpet; enter EUNUCH, in haste, carrying a small box)*

EUNUCH Girls, girls, fetch the queen. Tony approaches. *(enter CLEOPOTROAST wheeling in LASCIVIUS on a hand truck. SHE dumps him on the bed.)*

CHARMIAN Tony is here.

CLEOPOTROAST *(very dramatic)* And I've betrayed him. I must kill myself. And you, too, Lascivius. If only I could find my asp.

LASCIVIUS *(aside)* Hell, that's acting.

CHARMIAN You were playing with it in the garden.

CLEOPOTROAST Yes. I dug a hole and put my asp in it. My asp is the color of the Egyptian soil. Then I dug another hole and another.

CHARMIAN I know your problem.

LASCIVIUS So do I.

CLEOPOTROAST What is it?

LASCIVIUS You don't know your asp from a hole in the ground.

EUNUCH Do you speak true, queen? You'd take thy life?

CLEOPOTROAST Yes.

EUNUCH If only you could find your asp?

CLEOPOTROAST Yes.

EUNUCH Despair not, queen. Your asp is found.

CLEOPOTROAST It is?

EUNUCH I saw it in the garden and put it in this royal box.

169

CLEOPOTROAST Thanks a lot, buster.

EUNUCH *(taking asp from box, giving it to CHARMIAN)* Give the queen her asp.

(CHARMIAN takes the asp to her bosom. It bites. SHE passes the asp on to each GIRL who passes it on to the next. repeating in turn, "Give the queen her asp." The asp, of course, bites each GIRL in turn, and EACH in turn dies sighing. The effect is not unlike a row of dominoes. CLEOPOTROAST at last has the asp.)

CLEOPOTROAST *(holding asp)* Ah, the asp is in my grasp. Take it, Lascivius. We are the guilty pair. We must embrace death together. You first, of course. *(SHE tosses him the asp. HE gingerly catches it, keeping it at a distance.)*

LASCIVIUS. Nay, queen. 'Twould be bad manners to precede thee. *(HE tosses the asp back to CLEOPOTROAST. SHE catches it as before.)*

CLEOPOTROAST. *(through her teeth)* We don't stand on ceremony here. *(SHE tosses the asp back to him. HE catches it again.)*

LASCIVIUS But thy remains, oh, beauteous queen. Who will arrange them when thou kick'st the bucket?

CLEOPOTROAST I hadn't thought of that.

LASCIVIUS When Tony and Squeezer come, they must not see thee with thy make-up smudged. You go first. I'll fix thee up, then quickly follow.

CLEOPOTROAST Thou hast a point, Lascivius. Give me the asp. *(HE does. SHE presses it to her bosom.)* Ouch! The venom works. *(as if seeing a vision)* And even now, I'm at the gates of Heaven.

LASCIVIUS What dost thou see?

CLEOPOTROAST Look! All Olympus has lined up to greet me. Oh! what divine gods you Romans have! What heavenly biceps! *(now dying, SHE lapses into verse:)*
SWEET DEATH, I THANK THEE FOR 'TIS VERY CLEAR,
I'M REALLY GOING TO LIKE THE LIFE UP HERE.

(SHE dies with her rear end up in the air. Heroic, sentimental music begins here, underscoring LASCIVIUS's speech and swelling to the curtain.)

LASCIVIUS OH, EUNUCH, PLACE A WREATH UPON HER BROW.

(EUNUCH takes LASCIVIUS's wreath and puts it on CLEOPOTROAST's rear.)

THAT'S WHAT THE PUBLIC WANTS—NEW FACES NOW.

(The sound of a distant horn)

GREAT SQUEEZER COMES. SO, EUNUCH, LET'S SKEDAD-
DLE,
OR, WE'LL BE UP THE NILE WITHOUT A PADDLE.

EUNUCH BUT, NAY, THIS ENDING'S WRONG—INDEED,
GROTESQUE;
THIS QUEEN WILL LIVE FOREVER IN BURLESQUE.

LASCIVIUS QUITE RIGHT. UP, FRIENDS. NOW FAME IS IN
YOUR GRASP.

(All CORPSES rise.)

AND, CLEOPOTROAST, SHOW THE WORLD YOUR ASP.

BLACKOUT

That's what the public wants—new faces...

Monologues were called "Skull Lectures" by Burlesque comics. When all else failed—when, say, your straight man showed up for the matinee too drunk to perform—you could always lecture someone's skull. In other words, you could take a mute performer onto the stage—perhaps a dumb kid or sullen woman—and direct at your stooge a series of insult jokes.

Monologues, in other words, were only a last resort. Burlesque was situation humor, not stand-up comedy. Nevertheless, I wrote two skull lectures for Mickey Rooney, one for the original *Sugar Babies* and one for a proposed sequel.

In the 1979 show, the first-act finale was a tribute to a pioneer Burlesque troupe of the 1890's—Madame Rentz and her All-Female Minstrel Extravaganza. Mickey appeared as a broken-down chorus girl who, under prompting from the Interlocutor (Ann Miller), shared the story of her life and hard times with the audience.

In the sequel (not yet produced), the plan calls for the principal comic to appear as a woman—Petunia in "The Nursemaids." So this time his skull lecture in the first-act finale could not be a female impersonation. Instead I created a character for him based on Frank "Bring 'Em Back Alive" Buck, the great animal trainer. This device allowed me to make use of anthropomorphic animal stories that otherwise could not be dramatized.

The final joke in the animal sequence was told to me by my friend of twenty-five years, Maxie Furman, formerly the house comic at the Troc Theatre in Philadelphia and for four years the second banana in *Sugar Babies*. (He died during the national tour.)

Maxie was a kind and gentle man whose stage persona was brilliantly acerbic. As a raconteur and joke teller, he was without peer, and in these monologues his hand is everywhere.

MORE TO BE PETTED THAN CENSURED
("Hortense")

After FEMALE minstrel number, enter 1ST COMIC as HORTENSE, an aging chorus girl. HE wears a garish dress and blonde wig.

HORTENSE I'm sorry I'm late, Madame Interlocutor, but I was down at the docks again, saying farewell to the brave men who guard our shores.

INTERLOCUTOR That was kind of you, Countess.

HORTENSE It's my favorite charity—naval relief. *(a rattle of tambourines from the CHORUS)*

INTERLOCUTOR That's a beautiful dress you're wearing, Countess.

HORTENSE Yes, isn't it? *(lifts skirt to reveal a black garter)* What do you think of my garters? They cost me fifteen hundred francs in Paris.

INTERLOCUTOR Very racy. But your dress is so gay. Why are your garters black?

HORTENSE In memory of those who passed above. *(tambourines again)*

INTERLOCUTOR Ah, memories. I'm sure yours are legion. Would you care to share them with us, Countess?

HORTENSE I'll share my heartaches, yes.

INTERLOCUTOR It will ease the pain. *(INTERLOCUTOR moves U.S. to her appointed chair, as HORTENSE comes forward to tell her troubles to the audience. While HORTENSE speaks, the ORCHESTRA softly plays sentimental music.)*

HORTENSE My name is Hortense...Well, it is. I come from a large family. Fifteen in the family. All children. My father used to say to me, "Listen, Stupid." He always called me Listen. "Why don't you get a job? So at least we'll know what kind of work you're out of." I said,

173

"I've tried, papa, but life is hard. I'm gonna run away from home. I'm gonna run, do you hear?" And he said, "On your mark...get...set..." I joined a dance troupe. Well, I did. I danced on my right leg. I danced on my left leg, and between the two of them I made a lot of money. Our little troupe was invited to entertain the soldiers at Fort Knox. And the boys were so polite. I wore my most provocative dress. And when I walked through the barracks, all the privates stood up. The head Colonel fell in love with me. "Hortense," he said, "will you grace my presence at the military ball?" I said, "Silly goose! Of course, I will." He wore his medals, and I wore my organdy gown. We sipped champagne, and we danced. He held me close...closer...closer...and then he went off in his uniform, and I never saw him again. After I lost my colonel, life was a drag. Not that I lacked for lovers. There was old Judge Deadwood. He was sixty. I was twenty-two. "I'm a regular Don Juan," he said, and he spoke the truth. After one he was done. Then lightning struck. The once-in-a-lifetime man came into my life. Brock Allison, the Ketchup King. We met in a speakeasy. He poured me a glass of whiskey. "Say when," he said, and I said, "as soon as I finish the whiskey." It was a whirlwind courtship. And Brock was so generous in his own way. He asked me what I wanted for an engagment present. And I said, "Pearls...pearls...pearls." So he got me a bushel of oysters and wished me luck. And on our wedding day he gave me a nightgown with fur around the bottom. "What's the fur for?" I said. And he replied, "To keep your neck warm." That night when the wedding guests had gone, he took me tenderly in his arms. "Tell me, Hortense," he whispered. "Am I the first?" And I said, "Why does everybody ask me that?" For some reason Brock became moody; business took him to Europe. He deserted me. I was alone again. I was driven to drink. I forgot who drove me. I became a lush. The other day I was seated at a bar with my pet duck under my arm, and this drunk came up to me and said, "Hey, you! Where did you get that pig?" I said, "This isn't a pig." And he said, "I was talking to the duck." Years of heartbreak and despair followed. But all things pass. One day I was walking in the lobby of my hotel, and there he was again! Yes! You guessed. It was Brock talking to my old friend the Colonel. I laughed gaily. I didn't want them to see the cracks in my shattered heart. And I must have hidden my feelings pretty well. Because I overheard the Colonel say to Brock, "Is that Hortense?" And Brock replied, "She looks pretty relaxed to me." Brock said, "My darling, how wonderful to see you here in [LOCAL] after all these years. Tell me, what are you up to?" And I said, "Fifty dollars." Then Brock gave a little moan. "Oh, Hortense," he said, "can you ever forgive me for deserting you all those years ago?" And I told him a little poem that I had composed for just such an occasion.

THE MOON MAY KISS THE STARS ON HIGH;
THE BEE MAY KISS THE BUTTERFLY;
THE MORNING DEW MAY KISS THE GRASS,
AND YOU, DEAR BROCK, FAREWELL.

BLACKOUT

ANIMAL CRACKERS

Enter STRAIGHT as ZOO KEEPER.

STRAIGHT Ladies and gentlemen, the Gaiety Theatre is proud to present, as another added attraction, the world's greatest explorer and animal trainer, Mr. "Bring 'Em Back Alive" himself, Count _____. *(COMIC enters in safari outfit with pith helmet, etc.)*

COMIC Thank you. Just call me "Tex."

STRAIGHT All right. Tex has agreed to answer some questions, sharing with us his vast knowledge of the animal kingdom. But first we'd all like to know what part of Texas you are from.

COMIC I'm not from Texas. I'm from Louisiana.

STRAIGHT Then why do they call you Tex?

COMIC Well, it's better than Louise.

STRAIGHT It is at that. *(reads from card)* Mr. A. B. of [LOCAL] asks, "Is catching wild animals a dangerous profession?"

COMIC You bet it is. And if you don't believe me, ask my late wife.

STRAIGHT Your late wife?

COMIC Yes, she was my partner and assistant for many years.

STRAIGHT How did she die? Was she mauled by a tiger?

COMIC No, she was the victim of a fatal misunderstanding. We had pitched our tent in a jungle clearing near the headwaters of the Nile. It was very hot when we went to sleep, so she and I were both nude under the mosquito netting. In the middle of the night a party of hunters on safari burst into the clearing making a hell of a racket. My wife was startled. Without waiting to put a robe on, she ran out of the tent to see what was happening. The head of the hunting party called out to her. "Are you game?" "Yes," she said. So he shot her.

STRAIGHT Dear me. You don't hunt yourself, do you?

COMIC Never!

STRAIGHT Which brings me to a question from B. S. of [LOCAL]. To what do you attribute your success at controlling animals?

COMIC I talk to them.

STRAIGHT *(incredulous)* Talk to them?

COMIC Yes. I know all the major language groups. I speak fluent duck, for example, a smattering of pig and a whole lot of bull.

STRAIGHT I wish you'd have a word or two with my dog. He needs a talking to.

COMIC Dogs can't talk. If any dog tells you he can talk, he's lying.

STRAIGHT Mr. O. B. of [LOCAL] asks, "What is your favorite among all the animals you've trained?"

COMIC That's easy. My zebra Clarabel.

STRAIGHT What makes her special?

COMIC She was always friendly, gregarious and curious, so much so indeed, that it sometimes got her into trouble. I'll give you an example. I had her working in a mixed animal act for Ringling Brothers, and one day, she strained a tendon jumping through a hoop. I put her on a farm for a few weeks of rest and recuperation. Being a friendly little creature, she decided to introduce herself to all the farm animals. She walked over to a chicken and said: "Hello, I'm a zebra. Who are you?"

"I'm a chicken," said the chicken.

"What do you do?" asked Clarabel.

"I lay eggs," said the chicken.

"That's useful," said Clarabel. She saw a cow in the pasture. She skipped over to the cow.

"Hello," she said. "I'm a zebra. Who are you?"

"I'm a cow," said the cow.

"What do you do?" asked Clarabel.

"I give milk," said the cow.

"That must make you popular," said Clarabel. Out of the corner of her eye, she saw a bull in a neighboring field. She bounded over to the bull.

"Hello," said Clarabel. "I'm a zebra. Who are you?"

"I'm a bull," said the bull.

"What do you do?" asked Clarabel.

"Well," said the bull. "You take off those fancy pajamas, and I'll show you what I do."

Just call me Tex.

STRAIGHT So animals of different types can converse with one another?

COMIC Some can. Some can't. The ones that can often have a thick accent. Still, I know lots of animals who have friends from another species. For example, a horse and a mouse of my acquaintance are devoted to one another. Every year they go to the Animal Rights Convention in Chicago and share a hotel room to save money. They are the most unlikely pals. Very different personalities. The horse is a respectable family sort and the mouse something of a playboy, but they seem to get along. Last year, they were sitting in their hotel bar after a hard day of going to meetings when a beautiful giraffe walked in and ordered a drink.

"I'm going to make that girl," said the mouse.

The horse scoffed, but before long, the mouse took his drink to the other side of the bar, and the horse saw him in earnest conversation with the giraffe. And soon, they left together, while the horse went back to his room alone.

Eleven o'clock came and no little mouse. Twelve o'clock, one o'clock. Two o'clock. The horse began to get worried because Chicago is a dangerous town for a mouse. He was about to call the police when at three o'clock the mouse staggered in. The horse had never seen such a battered mouse in his life. He barely had enough strength to crawl onto the bed and collapse.

"What in the hell happened to you?" asked the horse.

"I had the night of nights," said the mouse. "Never has a mouse had such a night. First I kissed her. Then I screwed her. Then I kissed her. Then I screwed her. I kissed her; then I screwed her. I kissed...I must have run a thousand miles."

STRAIGHT Are you pulling my leg? Is that a true story?

COMIC Of course, it is. I had it straight from the horse's mouth.

STRAIGHT Mr. J. C. of [LOCAL] wants to know if you have a pet yourself?

COMIC You might call him a pet. I call him a companion.

STRAIGHT Is it a dog?

COMIC No.

STRAIGHT A cat?

COMIC I have a duck.

STRAIGHT A duck?

179

COMIC His name is Arnie.

STRAIGHT That's an unusual choice.

COMIC Yes, and the world doesn't know what to make of a non-conformist. I was walking my duck the other day, and I passed a movie theatre. It was showing a film I wanted to see. I went to buy a ticket. The cashier looked at Arnie and said, "You can't bring that animal in here!"

"Animal?" I said. "He's just a little duck. He read the book. He wants to see the movie."

"You can't bring him in here," she said, "and that's final."

Well, I really wanted to see that film. So, I slipped around the corner, opened my coat, unzipped and put Arnie inside my pants. I closed the zipper, buttoned my coat, went to the box office, bought a ticket and got inside without any trouble.

I was sitting next to two old ladies. Well, I didn't want my little duck to stifle, so I opened my zipper a few inches, and Arnie stuck his head out.

"Mabel," said one of the old ladies to her friend, "do you see what I see?"

"Ah," said Mabel, "you've seen one; you've seen them all."

"Yes," said the first, "but this one is eating my popcorn."

BLACKOUT

Blackouts were very useful in Burlesque. These short dramatized jokes helped vary the pace of the revue. Also, because they could be performed in front of a downstage drop with minimal props and scenery, blackouts could help cover a scene shift (in the days when Burlesque still had scenery to shift).

I have used some fifty blackouts in various productions of *Sugar Babies*. Here are fourteen of the most successful.

These brief scenes, like most good jokes, depend on a carefully controlled rhythm. Rhythm is not to be confused with timing. Every comic needs a sense of timing—how to wait until a laugh is just past its peak, but not too far past it, before sailing in with the next speech. Timing is an aspect of performance. Rhythm is a quality belonging to the joke itself.

Most jokes obey "the rule of three."—two set-ups and a punch line. They employ ritual repetition to create an expectation in the audience that is finally released in laughter. The first and penultimate blackouts in this sequence ("Bait" and "Monkey Business") are perfect examples of the rule of three and of an expectation fulfilled.

"Polar Peril," the second blackout here, is another matter altogether. It manipulates the audience response by setting up a familiar expectation (three igloos) only to catch the audience off-guard (the finish comes after the second). When it is performed, the audience takes a few seconds to realize that the joke is over, then explodes with laughter.

All these brief skits have the same subject matter as the longer scenes: domestic disputes, sex in all its forms, greed, pomposity, human stupidity. These are the eternal preoccupations of low comedy from Aristophanes to Red Skelton, from Rabelais to Bert Lahr, from Francesco Andreini to Billy Hagan.

FISHING
("Bait")

COMIC discovered C., fishing. HE casts without success.

COMIC I've spent all day fishing on this pier, and I haven't had a bite. Maybe I'm using the wrong bait. *(enter L., 1ST FISHERMAN. HE has a pole and six fish on a string. COMIC stops him.)* Pardon me, bud. Did you catch all those fish on this pier?

1ST FISHERMAN Sure did.

COMIC What did you use for bait?

1ST FISHERMAN Well, I happen to be a doctor. This morning I performed a tonsillectomy. I cut up the tonsils into little pieces, and I used them for bait.

COMIC *(as 1ST FISHERMAN exits)* Thank you, doctor. Well, I don't know where I'm going to get any tonsils. *(enter R., 2ND FISHERMAN, with rod and eight fish on a string. COMIC stops him.)* Hey, bud. Did you catch all those fish on this pier?

2ND FISHERMAN Bet your life I did.

COMIC What did you use for bait?

2ND FISHERMAN Well, you see, I happen to be a doctor. This morning I performed an appendectomy. I cut up the appendix into little pieces and used that for bait. *(2ND FISHERMAN exits.)*

COMIC Much obliged. *(to himself)* Tonsils, appendixes. Well, they're all catching fish. *(3RD FISHERMAN enters with more than a dozen fish on his string. As HE crosses, COMIC stops him.)* Oh, pardon me, doctor...

3RD FISHERMAN What doctor? I'm a rabbi.

BLACKOUT

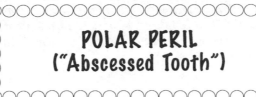

POLAR PERIL
("Abscessed Tooth")

Lights come up on a snowy-white expanse. We discover the COMMANDER (COMIC) tied to a stake with a signpost on it marked "North Pole." To L. of pole are three igloos. The COMMANDER is being menaced by an Eskimo WARRIOR (STRAIGHT). Sound effects of howling wind and wolves.

WARRIOR Commander, you have been sentenced to death for the capital crime of fishing in the Chief's ice-hole. There's only one way out. We Eskimos admire virility and courage. If you can pass the standard coming of age test which we give to all our warriors, we may let you escape with your life.

COMMANDER I'm good at taking tests. I'll take the test.

WARRIOR You see those three igloos over there? In the first igloo is a gallon of fermented blubber juice. It's about two hundred proof. You have ten seconds to drink that blubber juice without passing out. In the second igloo there's a ferocious polar bear. It weighs about half a ton, and it's got an abscessed tooth. You have fifteen seconds to pull that tooth and give that polar bear some relief. In the third tent there's a beautiful, unsoiled, untouched Eskimo girl. But she's got a bone knife in her right hand and a harpoon in her left, and she hates explorers. You have thirty seconds to throw her down and make a woman of her. *(WARRIOR cuts COMMANDER from the pole. Suspense music begins.)* Get going, Commander. Shake those legs of yours.

COMMANDER They're shaking. Everything's shaking. *(HE rushes into the first igloo, and we hear a gurgling noise.)*

WARRIOR That blubber juice is strong stuff. It made my sister grow hair. Too bad it was on her face. *(COMMANDER lurches from the tent, drunk.)* Well, hit me with an ice bucket, Commander. Three seconds. You broke the Arctic record.

COMMANDER, *(more than a little drunk)* Lead me to that polar bear. *(WARRIOR points to the second igloo. COMMANDER staggers to it.*

Melodramatic music builds. The igloo quakes. We hear screams of animal and human agony, giant roars, oaths and muffled execrations. COMMANDER slides out face first and is pulled back inside. Then, out of the tent comes the COMMANDER, bruised, battered and torn.) Now, where's that girl with the abscessed tooth?

BLACKOUT

You see those three igloos over there?

AN UNUSUAL PET
("Frog Story")

Well-dressed MAN discovered in front of low railing.

MAN Here's how it happened. Harry went to a pet store right before Christmas. As he was about to leave, he heard a little voice say, "Take me home. Take me home." He looked down, and there was a sweet little green frog with an imploring look on its face. Well, who could resist such a plea? He bought the frog, took it home and put it in an aquarium. "Aren't you going to take me to bed?" said the little voice. Well, it's important for a pet to feel loved and welcomed on its first night in a new home. So Harry picked the frog up and placed it on the pillow next to his head. "Aren't you going to kiss me goodnight?" said the frog. "Why not?" thought Harry. He leaned over and kissed those thin green lips. Then, suddenly there was a shimmer of light and a puff of smoke. And instead of the frog on Harry's pillow, there was a beautiful naked sixteen-year old girl. And that in summation, ladies and gentlemen of the jury, is my client's entire defense in this matter.

BLACKOUT

SNAPSHOTS
("Get It Enlarged")

Ten bars of the wedding march. BRIDE and GROOM appear.

GROOM Well, dear, at last we're married. But I have a confession to make. Two nights ago when we were staying at your mother's house—you in the one room and I in another—I decided I wanted a little peek, a preview. Well, you told me you never wore clothes to bed, so I sneaked into your room after you had fallen asleep, lifted up the covers and took a peek.

BRIDE Did you like what you saw?

GROOM I said to myself I wish I had a camera.

BRIDE What would you do?

GROOM I'd take a picture.

BRIDE Then what would you do?

GROOM I'd put it on the desk in my office and look at it all day long.

BRIDE I have a confession to make, too.

GROOM Is that so, dear?

BRIDE I wanted a little peek, a preview. Well, you never wear clothes to bed either. So last night after you'd fallen asleep, I sneaked into your room, lifted up the covers and took a peek.

GROOM Did you like what you saw?

BRIDE I said to myself, "I wish I had a camera."

GROOM What would you do?

BRIDE I'd take a picture.

GROOM Then what would you do?

BRIDE I'd get it enlarged.

BLACKOUT

I have a confession to make.

A CEMETERY WITH LIGHTS
("Philadelphia")

Spotlight discovers VILLAIN (STRAIGHT) in frock coat, standing over seated FATHER (CHARACTER MAN) near L. proscenium.

VILLAIN Well, the mortgage is three months overdue, and I won't wait a day longer.

FATHER Just give me a little more time. My daughter, Little Nell, is coming back today. And she promised she'd bring the money. *(auto horn offstage)* Here's Little Nell now. *(enter NELL, dressed modestly but attractively)* Oh, Nell, thank God you're here. The interest on the mortgage is due.

NELL Never mind the interest. How much is the principal?

VILLAIN Three thousand dollars.

NELL Here's your money. *(hands him money, takes paper from him, hands paper to FATHER)* Here's your mortgage. *(to VILLAIN again)* Now get. *(HE exits R.)*

FATHER Oh, Nell, I knew you wouldn't fail us. But where did you get the money?

NELL In Philadelphia.

FATHERIn Philadelphia? You got three thousand dollars in Philadelphia? Look at me, Little Nell, and tell me: have you been good?

NELL To get three thousand dollars in Philadelphia, you've got to be good.

BLACKOUT

TIT FOR TAT
("Post Office")

HUSBAND *discovered reading a newspaper. WIFE, wearing a shabby dress, enters.*

WIFE _____, you're the cheapest husband a girl ever had.

COMIC What do you mean, cheap? I bought you that dress, didn't I?

WIFE One dress! One dress! And look at it. Just for that, you can have it back. *(SHE takes off the dress and throws it at him. Now SHE stands before him in brief underwear. HE is still buried in the newspaper.)* Now, do you know what I'm going to do? I'm going to humiliate you. I'm going downtown, dressed exactly like this, where all your friends are, past the post office, and then the whole world will see exactly how cheap you are.

HUSBAND *(looking up from the paper)* You're going downtown?

WIFE Yes.

HUSBAND Dressed exactly like that?

WIFE Yes.

HUSBAND Where all my friends are?

WIFE Yes!

HUSBAND Past the post office?

WIFE Yes!!

HUSBAND *(handing her envelope)* Here, mail this letter.

BLACKOUT

189

Call the weather bureau.

WEATHER REPORT
("Coast Is Clear")

HUSBAND discovered, ready to leave on business trip, in overcoat, with suit-case nearby. WIFE in negligee. Telephone on stand.

WIFE Oh, darling, I think it's terrible—the boss sending you on a business trip only three days after our wedding.

HUSBAND Don't worry, dear. I'll be back before long. *(Phone rings. HUSBAND answers.)* What? Why ask me? Call the navy. *(HE hangs up. To WIFE)* Will you miss me when I'm not here?

WIFE Miss you? Darling, every second will be an eternity. I'll keep your picture next to my heart. *(Phone rings. HUSBAND answers.)*

HUSBAND Not you again? Buy a paper. Call the weather bureau. *(HE hangs up.)*

WIFE Who was that, dear?

HUSBAND Some damn fool wants to know if the coast is clear.

BLACKOUT

EXTRA HANDICAP
("Drag Herbert")

WOMAN discovered, fuming. MAN enters with golf clubs.

WOMAN This is the last straw, Edgar. You promised you'd be finished with your golf game by two o'clock, and it's after six.

MAN Don't yell at me, dear. I had a terrible day. On the third tee, Herbert, my best friend in the world, dropped dead as he started to swing.

WOMAN Oh, I'm sorry, dear. That must have been awful.

MAN Yes. All day long it was hit the ball, drag Herbert, hit the ball, drag Herbert.

BLACKOUT

A FUNEREAL MOOD
("Walk to the Cemetery")

A FATHER, his SISTER, her SON, his DAUGHTER discovered looking into an open coffin.

SON Poor old granddad. One of the most important people in the history of this town.

DAUGHTER What a prince of a fellow.

FATHER Let's make a big event out of his funeral. We'll have a thousand people, rent a hundred limos.

SISTER Why waste so much money? We'll have a few friends—and only one limo for the four of us.

SON Well, let's have a lot of flowers. Let's surround him with hundreds of lilies. He was a great man.

DAUGHTER A dozen lilies should be enough. Why waste the money?

SISTER To hell with the lilies. Save the money. Here's a rose.

   (GRANDPA'S CORPSE rises from the coffin.)

GRANDPA'S CORPSE Get me my pants. I'll walk to the cemetery.

BLACKOUT

**CLOSE SHAVE
("Manicurist")**

COMIC discovered in a barber chair, being shaved by a BARBER with a straight razor. A pretty MANICURIST is doing his nails.

COMIC Say, you're the prettiest young thing I've seen all week. How about a date tonight?

MANICURIST Oh, sir, I couldn't do that.

COMIC Why not? I'll take you to the hottest spot in town. Buy you the best dinner in the place. Then we'll dance cheek to cheek and go back to my place for a nightcap. We'll slip into something comfortable...

MANICURIST You don't understand, sir. I'm a married woman.

COMIC What difference does that make? Just tell your husband you're going out with a girlfriend.

MANICURIST Tell him yourself. He's shaving you.

BLACKOUT

SELF-DETERMINATION
("Boxing Blackout")

BOXER enters, shadow-boxing. TRAINER is beside him.

BOXER I almost had him, Butch.

TRAINER Yeah, you took him by surprise. He thought he'd killed you. Let's face it, kid, it's time to retire.

BOXER Just one more fight.

TRAINER There's no one left. You've lost to everyone.

BOXER There's Murphy.

TRAINER You can't fight Murphy.

BOXER Murphy's a bum. I know I could beat Murphy.

TRAINER You can't fight Murphy.

BOXER I'll murder him. I'll knock him to smithereens. He's no good. Bring on Murphy!

TRAINER You can't fight Murphy!

BOXER Why not?

TRAINER You're Murphy.

BLACKOUT

THE OTHER SIDE
("Happy Medium")

Discovered: MOUSAKA and RICH LADY at table with crystal ball between them.

RICH LADY So, you're the famous Madame Mousaka?

MOUSAKA Yes, I am the great Mousaka, the original happy medium.

RICH LADY Can you really put someone in touch with a person from the other side?

MOUSAKA When I'm dealing with a true believer.

RICH LADY Oh, I believe. I'll pay you anything if you succeed. But don't deceive me. If you do, you'll quickly see me strike a happy medium.

MOUSAKA Whom are you trying to reach?

RICH LADY My late husband, Pierpont Whitney III.

MOUSAKA (*going into a trance*) Are you there, Pierpont Whitney III? Someone wants to speak to you. Speak, oh, immortal spirit. Your wife is waiting.

VOICE OF WHITNEY (*off*) Is that you, Gladys?

RICH LADY That's him. I know his voice. Yes, it's me, Poopsie. Tell me, dear, what is it like on the other side?

VOICE OF WHITNEY (*off*) It's wonderful, Gladys. All I do is eat and make love. Eat and make love. Eat and make love.

RICH LADY Is that what heaven's like?

VOICE OF WHITNEY (*off*) Heaven? I'm a bull in Montana.

BLACKOUT

196

MONKEY BUSINESS
("Regular Price")

In front of a traveler, spotlight picks up POLICEMAN and SOUBRETTE next to an open window. SHE is wearing the POLICEMAN's coat and apparently nothing else. HE is in shirt sleeves, taking notes.

SOUBRETTE Thank you, officer, for lending me your coat. It was getting very drafty up here.

POLICEMAN You're welcome, Miss. Now, can you tell me just what happened here?

SOUBRETTE Well, my boss, Mr. Gilmore, just jumped out of the window, and it's twenty stories down.

POLICEMAN Who are you?

SOUBRETTE I'm his private secretary. I take dictation. I type. I lick stamps.

POLICEMAN Was there anything odd about Mr. Gilmore's behavior today?

SOUBRETTE Well, he was always a bit peculiar. I had only been working here three days when he burst into the office one morning in a terrible state. "Miss Jones," he said, "you're the most beautiful creature I've ever seen in my life. If I give you a hundred dollars, will you stand before me in your slip? I promise you, there'll be no monkey business." Well, officer, to a working girl a hundred dollars is a lot of money.

POLICEMAN Of course, it is.

SOUBRETTE So I took the money and stood before him in my slip.

POLICEMAN Was he as good as his word?

SOUBRETTE Yes, there was no monkey business.

POLICEMAN Did that satisfy him?

SOUBRETTE It did until a week ago.

POLICEMAN What happened then?

SOUBRETTE He burst into the office again, and he was a sorry sight. His tie was askew; his eyes were rimmed with red. "Miss Jones," he said, "I can't get your face out of my mind. If I give you two hundred dollars, will you stand before me in your panties and your brassiere? I promise there'll be no monkey business." Well, officer, to a working girl, two hundred dollars is a lot of money.

POLICEMAN Of course, it is.

SOUBRETTE So I took the money and stood before him in my panties and brassiere.

POLICEMAN Was he as good as his word?

SOUBRETTE Yes, there was no monkey business.

POLICEMAN Did that satisfy him?

SOUBRETTE Until ten minutes ago.

POLICEMAN What happened then?

SOUBRETTE Oh, he pushed open the door, and he looked just awful. "Miss Jones," he said. "I'm spending sleepless nights because of you. If I pay you five hundred dollars, will you stand before me in the nude? I promise there'll be no monkey business." Well, officer, to a working girl, five hundred dollars is a lot of money.

POLICEMAN Of course, it is.

SOUBRETTE So I removed my clothes and stood before him in the nude. "Miss Jones," he said, "I can't stand it anymore. How much is the monkey business?"

POLICEMAN Yes?

SOUBRETTE And when I told him my regular price was ten dollars, he jumped out of the window.

BLACKOUT

DUTIFUL DAUGHTERS
("Chuck")

A FATHER discovered in a rocking chair reading a newspaper. THREE GIRLS in gingham dresses next to him. The GIRLS clear their throats to get his attention.

FATHER Yes, what is it, girls?

ALL THREE GIRLS FATHER, DEAR FATHER, DON'T STAY UP
    LATE.
    IT'S FRIDAY NIGHT, AND WE EACH HAVE A DATE.

1ST GIRL I HAVE A DATE WITH A GUY NAMED JOE.
    HE'S TAKING ME TO A PICTURE SHOW.

FATHER *(abstractedly)* Have a good time, dear. *(1ST GIRL curtsies and exits.)*

2ND GIRL I HAVE A DATE WITH A GUY NAMED PETE.
    WE'RE GOING TO THE RITZ TO GET SOMETHING TO EAT.

FATHER Have a good time, dear. *(2ND GIRL curtsies and exits.)*

3RD GIRL I HAVE A DATE WITH A GUY NAMED CHUCK...

FATHER *(angrily dropping paper)* You get right upstairs and go to bed.

BLACKOUT

AFTERWORD

Sugar Babies was nominated for eight Tonys and didn't win a single one. It will never win an award. The Broadway intellectuals (now there's an oxymoron) who vote on these matters are middle-brows through and through.

So I will not be given the chance to make a thank-you speech, praising all the people who helped shape this cheerful entertainment. I had many brilliant collaborators—the late Harry Rigby, Ernest Flatt, Toni Kaye, Rudi Tronto, David Campbell, Arthur Malvin and, of course, Mickey Rooney, Ann Miller, Ann Jillian, Jane Summerhays, Eddie Bracken and Rip Taylor. All these people helped create a show that was entertaining in the present and respectful of the past.

I have already paid tribute to the four great comedians who in my youth educated me to the joys of Burlesque—Billy Hagan, Billy Foster, Bert Carr and Maxie Furman.

There were many other variety actors from whom I learned: Bob Ferguson, a droll comedian who proved to me that low comedy does not have to be loud or overbearing. Also Jimmy Matthews, Billy "Zoot" Reed, Charley Robinson, Billy Ainsley, Hap Hyatt, Irving Benson, Steve Mills, Al Anger, Lou Ascol and Joe De Rita—top bananas everyone of them.

Irving Harmon was also a mentor of mine. He was the wisest, most articulate comic of them all. Also the saddest. He despised his life in the slum music halls, and he killed himself before he reached his forty-fifth birthday.

I remember great straight men also: Dick Dana, Danny Jacobs, Lee Clifford and Al Baker among them. Then there were the superb talking women: Grace Reed, Barbara Curtis and Nikki Vela.

Oh! to see them all perform again. What a show that would be!

Oh! to see them all perform again.

APPENDIX

Sources and Related Entertainments

1. A MINSTREL SOURCE FOR BURLESQUE BITS

Frank Dumont was a prolific writer of variety sketches and minstrel afterpieces. One of his most successful, "The Sulphur Cure," is a source for many of the standard doctor scenes. A perceptive reader will notice that I borrowed one of Dumont's jokes for "The Transformer."

THE SULPHUR CURE

(a minstrel show afterpiece by Frank Dumont, 1881)

A chamber with doors and a window. A table and chair R. Large screen L. There is a bath box C. and a club and bottle on the table. DOCTOR DRAKE is discovered at the table.

Note: The bath box is arranged as follows. It is about five feet high and four feet long. The back of the box is formed by the upstage flat, and there is an escape built into the flat. Inside the box is a huge skeleton on wires, and also a pair of dummy feet and a dummy head. There is a giant wheel on the L. corner of the box and a spigot to which a hose can be attached. If a wired skeleton should prove too difficult to rig, substitute a man in a skeleton suit dressed in such a way as to appear headless.

DOCTOR Oh, dear. Five o'clock, and no one has called to take one of my revolutionary new sulphur baths. I can't understand it. I advertised in all the daily papers. *(HE picks up paper and reads from it.)* "Dr. Drake's Satisfying Sulphur Cure: A Sovereign Remedy, Restorative and Panacea. Guaranteed effective for Rheumatism, Kidney Stones, Heart Disease and Lung Spots. Straightens hair, flushes out Flu and wards off Warts. Reasonable Terms for Daily Treatments." The style is perfect, the adjectives beyond compare. And still I haven't had a single cash customer. *(HE looks at watch again.)* By the way, where is my slow-witted attendant? Dick. Dick. Do you hear me calling you?

> *(DICK, his bedraggled rascal of an assistant, enters eating a piece of bread.)*

DICK Here I am, Doctor Drake.

DOCTOR You lazy vagabond, where have you been?

DICK I was sleeping in the pantry.

DOCTOR Good God, Dick. Business has never been worse, yet you keep eating.

DICK It's a habit I got into.

DOCTOR Curb your appetite, my boy. If you don't, we'll all be bankrupt.

DICK You promised me a slice of bread for every patient.

DOCTOR And we haven't had a patient in a week. You're taking your fees in advance.

DICK You say I have fleas in my pants?

DOCTOR No. Fees. Fees! You're eating me out of house and home.

DICK It's not my fault I get hungry. Besides, I got a bone to pick with you.

DOCTOR What's that?

DICK You said if I worked for just my room and board, you'd teach me doctoring.

DOCTOR Didn't I give you a book just last week? Dr. Mekum's Manual of Medicine and Quick Cure Cyclopedia.

DICK You did, and I been readin' it regular.

DOCTOR It's not enough to read it, Dick. You got to memorize the remedies. That's the only way to pass the licensing exam.

DICK I been memorizin' every chance I get. Look, I'll prove it to you. Ask me somethin', anything at all.

DOCTOR Anything at all?

DICK Do your worst.

DOCTOR All right, Dick. Let's see. Tell me what's the best cure for insomnia?

DICK The best cure for insomnia is a good night's sleep.

DOCTOR Pretty good, son. Now here's a hard one. Supposin' a man has a cold. How do you keep it from reaching his chest?

DICK That's simple. You jest tie a knot in his neck.

DOCTOR Well, you're not quite ready, Dick, but you're getting there. Keep it up. Before you know it, you'll be practicin'. *(loud knock at the door)* Ah, a knock. Run quickly and see who it is. Maybe it's a cash customer for my sulphur cure. *(DICK opens door and admits SAMPSON CHICKWEED who carries a huge umbrella, carpetbag and parcels.)*

DICK Come in, sir, come in. Take off your hat. *(HE knocks off SAMPSON's hat.)*

SAMPSON My name is Sampson Chickweed, I'd like to see Dr. Duck.

DICK The ducks are all out. There's a Dr. Drake here though. He's an old quack.

DOCTOR *(to SAMPSON)* My dear sir, what can I do for you?

SAMPSON I read your advertisement—about the vapor and the sulphur baths.

DOCTOR Ah, good. Good! What are your symptoms?

SAMPSON I have trouble breathing.

DOCTOR Well, I can stop that. Anything else?

SAMPSON Yes. Some years ago, I was kicked by a mule and sustained a compound fraction of the knee pan. When I saw your notice in the paper it gave me hope.

DOCTOR And well it might.

SAMPSON *(eagerly)* I can't wait to try your treatment.

DICK Take your time. He'll scald you soon enough.

DOCTOR Quiet, Dick.

SAMPSON How much do you charge for a bath?

DOCTOR Ten dollars for the first bath and seven dollars for the second bath.

SAMPSON I'll take the second one.

DOCTOR Give me your carpetbag. Someone might steal it while you're bathing.

SAMPSON No, sir. I'll take care of it myself.

DICK It's five dollars extra if you take the bag into the bath. *(grabs at bag)*

DOCTOR Stop, Dick. Allow the gentleman to retain his property. *(to SAMPSON)* Take it with you to the bath, sir.

DICK *(whispering)* Don't forget the fleas in his pants.

SAMPSON What?

DOCTOR My assistant means that we always get our fees in advance.

SAMPSON *(paying him)* Here you are.

DOCTOR Good. Now step behind the screen and take your clothes off.

SAMPSON All right, doctor.

DOCTOR Dick, hurry downstairs and turn on the steam.

DICK *(exits)* Right you are, boss. *(SAMPSON gets behind screen while the DOCTOR opens up the box. SAMPSON throws coat, vest, pants, etc. over the screen.)*

DOCTOR *(adjusting dials on box)* What took you so long to get here, Mr. Chickweed? It's five o'clock. We were just closing up.

SAMPSON *(behind screen, undressing)* Well, I had trouble making up my mind. You see, my cousin was a patient of yours, and he said something which made me hesitate.

DOCTOR What did he say? Don't spare my feelings.

SAMPSON He said, "You gotta watch out for that Dr. Drake. If he treats you for liver trouble, you'll die of indigestion." *(emerges from behind the screen. HE is dressed in a white nightgown.)*

DOCTOR That's a slander, sir, and you can tell your cousin so. If I treat you for liver trouble, you'll die of liver trouble.

SAMPSON Now, doctor, where do I go?

DOCTOR Into this box. When the steam gets too hot, just cry out, and I'll shut it off. *(DICK enters and begins attaching a hose to the nozzle on the box.)*

SAMPSON *(stepping into the box)* Oh, I'm feeling warm already.

DICK You'll feel a lot warmer in a minute.

(The DOCTOR locks the box and adjusts SAMPSON's head, so that it fits through the opening and is fixed firmly in place. SAMPSON's feet—which are really a pair dummy feet—protrude from the box. The DOCTOR seizes them and also locks them firmly in place, preventing their withdrawal.)

SAMPSON Now, doctor, don't turn on too much steam. *(DOCTOR starts turning the wheel.)*

DOCTOR I'm an expert on these matters, sir. *(to DICK)* Come, Dick, help me with this wheel. *(DICK helps him.)*

SAMPSON Doctor, it's getting very hot in here.

DOCTOR Don't be a baby, Mr. Chickweed. You can stand another ten degrees. Look after him, Dick. I'll be back in a moment. *(DOCTOR exits.)*

DICK *(turning the wheel)* How do you feel now?

SAMPSON I'm fairly broiling.

DICK Nonsense. You're still six degrees cooler than the Bronx in August. *(turns wheel again)*

SAMPSON Every bone in my body aches.

DICK Then just be glad you ain't a herring. *(DICK begins searching through SAMPSON's pockets.)*

SAMPSON What are you doing with my clothes?

DICK Looking for fleas in your pants.

SAMPSON Doctor. Doctor. Your boy is robbing me.

DICK No, I ain't. *(turns wheel)*

SAMPSON Help. Help. Listen. You can have the clothes. Just turn the heat off and call the doctor.

DICK You're a tough case. I'll have to give you more vapor. *(turns wheel)*

SAMPSON I'm burning up.

DICK No, you ain't. We melted three men in that box yesterday. You ain't even half liquefied. *(turns wheel)*

SAMPSON Give me a drink, before I die of thirst.

DICK Here you are. *(gives him a vial of liquid from the table)*

SAMPSON *(sputtering)* What was that?

DICK Fusil oil and gunpowder. You'll explode any minute. I'm glad you brought this carpetbag. It's just what I needed. *(turns wheel)*

SAMPSON If you cook me, I'll come back to haunt you.

DICK I ain't afraid of ghosts, especially roasted ones. *(HE pours a glass of water on SAMPSON's feet. Steam sizzles and rises from them.)* You're getting cool. You could use another dose of sulphur. *(turns wheel)*

(Thrilling music underscores this action. SAMPSON yells lustily. DICK throws a cloth over his head. The cloth hides the substitution of a dummy head for SAMPSON's. The actor unseen by the audience, escapes through a secret exit in the flat. DICK gives the wheel several rapid turns. SAMPSON curses him furiously. DICK picks up the club from the table and taps the fake head presumably to shut SAMPSON up. The head falls off and rolls onto the floor. DICK drops the club, dismayed.)

DICK I've knocked his head off. What will I do? I know. Melt him down before the doctor comes.

(HE turns the wheel rapidly. There is a terrific crash, then an explosion inside the box. The box flies open and a huge headless skeleton emerges from it and walks towards DICK, as if to embrace him. Music. Smoke. Flame reflections. Either the skeleton embraces DICK or chases him up the aisle of the theatre.)

BLACKOUT

2. BITS FROM THE HONKY TONKS

(Stock speeches used frequently in Burlesque)

Burlesque comedians and straight men memorized standard cross-talk conversations that could be added to any scene. Everyone in the business knew these bits, and if one of the actors said the first line, the team could proceed to the finish without a stumble.

"Deductions," for example, could be used in any sketch in which the comic is employed by the straight man. And in any betting scene, the straight man would be happy to change the comic's hundred dollar bill.

DEDUCTIONS

A large blackboard, an easel chalk and some stage money.

COMIC Look, I been working for you a long time now, and I've decided to quit. Gimme my money.

STRAIGHT What do you mean, quit? Why?

COMIC Cause you ain't paid me, that's why.

STRAIGHT You mean I forgot to pay you?

COMIC I mean you ain't paid me nothing yet.

STRAIGHT Just how long have you been working for me?

COMIC A whole year—365 days. That's how long.

STRAIGHT And how much was I paying you?

COMIC Five dollars a day, and you owe me $1825. So come on, fork over. Let's have it, and I'll be on my way.

STRAIGHT How do you know I owe you that much?

COMIC Because I stayed up all night, and I figured it out. That's how I know, and I used up three sides of my room doing it.

STRAIGHT Well, I'm not going to take your word for it. I'll figure it out for myself! *(ignoring him, goes to blackboard which is set up facing audience)* Now let me see. There are 356 days in a year. *(puts down "365")*

COMIC Now, just multiply that by five.

STRAIGHT Just a minute. I'm not gonna pay you for something that you didn't do. How many hours a night did you sleep?

COMIC Eight hours.

STRAIGHT Eight hours, eh? You don't expect me to pay you while you're sleeping, do you?

COMIC Well, I thought maybe you would.

STRAIGHT Well, I'm not. Now, let me see. Eight hours a night for 365 nights, that makes 122 days you didn't work, so I'll just deduct 122 from 365 *(writing as HE talks)* and that leaves 243. Now—

COMIC Now, let's multiply.

STRAIGHT Oh, no, not yet. Now you work eight hours, and you sleep eight hours. What do you do with the other eight hours? *(COMIC goes through business of acting very shyly as if hiding something.)* Well, come on, what do you do? You don't do anything for me.

COMIC *(very shyly)* W-e-l-l...sometimes I think about you.

STRAIGHT Well, you don't work, that's for sure so I'm not gonna pay, am I? That means there's another 122 days, so I'll just deduct that ...122 from 243 *(doing so)*, and that leaves 121. Now we're getting some place!

COMIC Gee, I never lost money so fast in my whole life.

STRAIGHT Now...

COMIC Let's multiply.

STRAIGHT Just a minute. How much time do I give you for lunch every day?

COMIC An hour.

STRAIGHT An hour. Well...you don't expect me to pay you when you're eating?

COMIC N-o-o-ooo!

STRAIGHT An hour a day for a year is fifteen days.

COMIC Do I eat that much a year?

STRAIGHT Yes, sir, and I don't intend paying you for it.

COMIC Let's multiply for a change.

STRAIGHT Not yet.

COMIC Look, I'll settle for a quarter.

STRAIGHT *(ignoring him as HE writes)* Now deduct 15 from 121...that leaves 106...Now!

COMIC It ain't gonna be long now...

STRAIGHT You never worked for me on Sundays, did you?

COMIC *(wearily)* No.

211

STRAIGHT Well, you don't expect me to pay you for a day you didn't work, do you?

COMIC Absolutely not!

STRAIGHT Okay, then. Now there are 52 Sundays in a year, so I'll just deduct 52 from 106 *(writing)*, and that leaves 54...Now...

COMIC Yeah, NOW...now, I can see already I ain't gonna have enough money to get out of town.

STRAIGHT Now we come to Saturday.

COMIC What detained you?

STRAIGHT According to the union, you can't work but half a day on Saturday, so that leaves another 26 days that I'm not gonna pay you for, am I? S-o-o, I'll just deduct 26 from 54 *(writing)* which leaves 28...Now...

COMIC *(getting on his knees in prayer-like attitude)* Look, on my bended knees, I ask you to do somethin' for me.

STRAIGHT What is it?

COMIC *(pleadingly)* M-u-l-t-i-p-l-y.

STRAIGHT *(ignoring him)* Every year you take a two-week vacation on your own, that right? *(COMIC nods meekly in assent.)* Well, I'm not gonna pay you while you're on a vacation, am I? No! *(As HE says "No!" the COMIC is about to answer, but gets beaten to the answer, gets caught with his mouth open in a "take.")* So, that's another fourteen days I don't pay you for. Now 14 from 28 *(writing)* leaves 14, so I'll just deduct that...Now...

COMIC It's too bad there ain't more days in a year!

STRAIGHT Now, there are 13 legal holidays each year that you don't work on, such as New Year's, Abraham Lincoln's birthday, George Washington's birthday, the Fourth of July, Labor Day, Election Day, Thanksgiving, Columbus Day, Christmas Day *(or any other holidays like Garbage Day, Father's Day, Mother's Day, Latrine Day, etc.)* Well, anyway, there are 13 of them in all, and I'm not paying you for them!

COMIC And to think I used to wait for them days to come around.

STRAIGHT *(writing)* So 13 from 14 leaves one day. That's what I owe you for, one day. Never let it be said that I don't pay my debts. One times five is five, that's what I owe you. Five dollars, and here you are. *(paying him)*

COMIC *(taking it and looking at it)* I ain't crowding you, am I?

STRAIGHT Not at all. Keep it.

COMIC Look, I don't wanna beat you. Here, you take it.

STRAIGHT Why, what's the matter?

COMIC You forgot Chinese New Year!

BLACKOUT

CHANGING A HUNDRED

COMIC Pardon me, but have you got change for a hundred dollar bill?

STRAIGHT A hundred dollar bill? Oh, sure. *(takes the bill, pulls out a roll of money from pocket and starts to peel off the change)* Here you are. One...two...three...four...five...by the way, how old are you?

COMIC Twenty-one.

STRAIGHT *(continues counting)* 21...22...23...24...25. How old is your father?

COMIC Fifty-eight.

STRAIGHT *(counting)* 58, 59, 60, 61, 62. And how old is your grandmother?

COMIC Seventy.

STRAIGHT *(counting)* 70, 71, 72, 73, 74. How old is your grandfather?

COMIC Ninety-six.

STRAIGHT *(counting)* 96, 97, 98, 99 and 100. There you are, and here's two dollars extra for yourself!

BLACKOUT

3. A SOURCE FOR "WHO'S ON FIRST?"

"Who Dyed," an ancient scene, which can be traced at least as far back as 1905, is the source not only of Abbott and Costello's famous sketch, but also of another standard bit, "Flugel Street."

THE CLEANING AND DYEING SHOP
("Who Dyed?")

1ST COMIC meets 2ND COMIC on the street.

1ST COMIC Hello, _____.

2ND COMIC Hello, _____.

1ST COMIC I had a strange experience yesterday on my way to work.

2ND COMIC Really?

1ST COMIC You know that hotel at 9th and Arch? Well, it caught fire. I heard someone holler, "Save me. Save me." There was a woman on the fourth floor standing on the sill. I looked up and saw her predicament.

2ND COMIC Through all that smoke?

1ST COMIC Yes. I can spot them all right. I saw one on the other side of the Delaware River once. Almost drowned getting to her.

2ND COMIC What about the girl at the hotel?

1ST COMIC What about her?

2ND COMIC What did you do after you saw her predicament?

1ST COMIC I let the fireman handle it. I was late for work.

2ND COMIC You've got a job? That's a surprise. Where are you working?

1ST COMIC At the Market Street Cleaners and Dyers.

2ND COMIC What do you do there?

1ST COMIC I dye.

2ND COMIC You what?

1ST COMIC I dye for a living. If I don't dye, I can't live.

2ND COMIC Are you sick?

1ST COMIC No. You don't have to be sick to dye.

2ND COMIC You don't?

1ST COMIC In fact, if you're sick, you can't dye.

2ND COMIC How long have you been dying?

1ST COMIC About two years. My father dyed ten years before I was born.

2ND COMIC Well, if you're dying, what are you doing here?

1ST COMIC I took a day off. You can't dye every day, you know. It wears you out.

2ND COMIC So, you didn't feel like dying today?

1ST COMIC No. You see, I'm not dyeing for myself.

2ND COMIC You're dying for another fellow?

1ST COMIC Uh huh.

2ND COMIC Why doesn't the other fellow die himself?

1ST COMIC He doesn't have to. He's the boss. Others dye for him.

2ND COMIC What's the name of the man you work for?

1ST COMIC Who.

2ND COMIC The man you work for?

1ST COMIC Who.

2ND COMIC The man you work for?

1ST COMIC Who.

2ND COMIC Your boss. Look, you get paid, don't you?

1ST COMIC Of course. Don't you think I'm worth it?

2ND COMIC Who gives you the money?

1ST COMIC Naturally.

2ND COMIC Naturally?

1ST COMIC Naturally.

2ND COMIC So you get the money from Naturally?

1ST COMIC No.

2ND COMIC Then who gives it to you?

1ST COMIC Naturally.

2ND COMIC Naturally. That's what I said.

1ST COMIC No, you didn't! No, you didn't!

2ND COMIC You get the money from Naturally.

1ST COMIC But I don't!

2ND COMIC Then, you get the money from who?

1ST COMIC Naturally.

2ND COMIC What is the name of the man you get the money from?

1ST COMIC No. What's the bookkeeper.

2ND COMIC I don't know.

1ST COMIC She's the secretary.

BLACKOUT

4. VAUDEVILLE CROSS TALK

As Brooks McNamara correctly points out: "Underlying all of [the] complicated trade-offs and transformations [in the various branches of the variety stage] is a shared body of traditional stock material."

Take, for example, the vaudeville team of Moran and Mack, who played the Keith-Albee and Pantages Circuits with an act called "Two Black Crows." The blackface routines that these two men performed were based on an earlier minstrel act of Billy Kersand's. And who knows where he got the material from.

Burlesque comedians imitated the cross-talk formula of Moran and Mack, sometimes translating the Negro material into Dutch, Irish or Hebrew dialect. These ethnic clowns were the principal stock characters of the early days of Vaudeville and Burlesque. In Burlesque, at least, the foreign accents disappeared shortly after the beginning of the first World War.

Here is a Vaudeville turn by Moran and Mack, climaxed by a famous tongue-twister speech spoken rapidly by Mack. Many Burlesque comedians borrowed this speech and delivered it, but without burnt cork to hide behind.

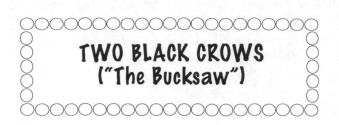

TWO BLACK CROWS
("The Bucksaw")

MORAN Well, with the minstrel show busted, I'm goin' back on my father's farm.

MACK Yes, that's all right for you, but what's gonna become of me?

MORAN Any place I go you are always welcome.

MACK Oh, I know that.

MORAN Yes, sir. Father says there's always a bed there for you.

MACK Your father's all right. But, I figured on doin' a little eatin', too.

MORAN Didn't my father feed you well the last time you were there?

MACK Your father didn't give me anything to eat. He just showed me a rabbit track and said, "Breakfast is on the other end." And doggone it, didn't I nearly run myself to death?

MORAN Well, father just wanted you to earn your breakfast. That's all.

MACK Your father's too stingy.

MORAN My father's not stingy; he's just economical.

MACK Yeah. That must be a new name for bein' tight.

MORAN Oh, my father's not tight.

MACK Why, your father is closer than the next minute.

MORAN Why, he's so generous he has spent $11.00 in five years.

MACK Oh, that ain't nothin', Willy. I got a brother so economical he ain't spent a cent in fifteen years.

MORAN No?

MACK No. But he'll be out next Thursday.

MORAN You shouldn't talk that way about my father, 'cause he's got religion.

MACK Yeah. And I'll bet if he has, he's got it in your ma's name.

MORAN Yeah, but my pa was mighty good to you when you was one of his pupils.

MACK Oh, your pa may be all right, but I couldn't use him. All he did was give me hard examples, and if I couldn't do them he'd put me in the dumb seat.

MORAN That's where you belong. It took you four weeks to learn how to spell stovepipe, and now you can't spell it.

MACK Who can't spell stovepipe?

MORAN Go on. Let me hear you spell it.

MACK Stovepipe?

MORAN Yeah, stovepipe.

MACK Stovepipe. Say, brother, can you spell it?

MORAN Sure I can spell it.

MACK Well, then, why, why you askin' me?

MORAN I want to see if you can spell it.

MACK Oh, I can spell it all right. Let me see now. Stovepipe! Stovepipe! Doggone it, that's easy, Willy. C'mon, give me something harder.

MORAN No, I want to hear you spell stovepipe.

MACK Let's see. D-o-d-o-g-c-o-s-t-cap-cap. How's that, Willy?

MORAN That's fine. Now spell stovepipe.

MACK Doggone. You're bound to have you a stovepipe, ain't ya, huh? Let me see now, stovepipe. Widgy, y-p-e-p-i-pipe.

MORAN What's that squiggy, widgy p-i-p-e for?

MACK Well, that's for the elbows, joints and ribs.

MORAN Well, Amos, I'll see you subsequently.

MACK No. If you see me it will be accidentally 'cause I got to go down to the hot house now.

MORAN What are you gonna do down there?

MACK Oh, I just wanna find out why blackbirds are red. *(music)* Look here at this newspaper, Willy. This is the funniest thing I ever saw. Doggone, look at the man comin' out of the house walkin' on his head.

MORAN A man comin' out of the house on his head?

MACK Yeah. There it is. Right there.

MORAN Let's see. Oh, you got that newspaper upside down.

MACK What you know about that, huh?

MORAN Is that all you have to do is sit there and laugh at cartoons in the newspaper?

MACK Oh, I like them.

MORAN Do you realize that all the money we have in the world is one five-cent piece?

MACK Well, why didn't the barber pay you?

MORAN Because I didn't know any better than to take you down to the barber shop where I was workin' and get you a job as a partner.

MACK Yeah, and I like that job.

MORAN The minute my back was turned you drank all the hair tonic.

MACK Yeah, but I didn't eat the soap.

MORAN No, because there was no soap there.

MACK Oh, now...

MORAN And another thing. What was you idea arguin' with that head barber?

MACK I, I wasn't arguin' with him, but he was eatin' garlic.

MORAN What does a man eatin' garlic have to do with you arguin' with him?

MACK Well, he asked me if I wanted a close shave, and when I smelled the garlic, I said, "No. Stand as far away as possible." And you know, Willy, that barber reminded me of the time I was livin' on the farm. I had a hired man workin' for me by the name of Esau Buck. One day I said to Esau, I said, "Esau, I'm goin' to town today. While I'm gone I want you to saw the wood and keep the old buck ram out of the garden." So, after I'd gone to town, Esau went out to saw the wood and when he saw the saw he thought he couldn't saw with that saw, so he looked around for another saw, but that was the only saw he saw so he wouldn't saw. Well, the next day I went to town and bought a new bucksaw for Esau Buck, and when I came home I hung the new bucksaw on the sawbuck by the seesaw. About that time, Esau Buck saw the old buck out in the garden eating cabbage, and while walking from the garden to the barn, the old buck saw the new bucksaw on the sawbuck by the seesaw. Now, when the old buck saw Esau Buck looking at the new bucksaw on the sawbuck by the seesaw, he made a dive for Esau Buck and missed Esau and hit the seesaw and knocked the seesaw against Esau Buck who fell over the bucksaw on the sawbuck by the seesaw. Now, I saw the old buck make a dive for Esau Buck and hit the seesaw and knock the seesaw against Esau Buck who fell over the bucksaw on the sawbuck by the seesaw. I picked up the ax to kill the old buck. But he saw me comin', pounded on my stomach, knocked me over the seesaw into Esau Buck who broke the bucksaw and the sawbuck and the seesaw and that's why Esau Buck don't work for us no more.

BLACKOUT

Matinee at the Old Howard

A FLEA IN HER REAR
(or ANTS IN HER PANTS)

Translated by Norman R. Shapiro

"THESE TRANSLATIONS ARE AS LIGHT AS AIR."

—THE NEW YORK TIMES BOOK REVIEW

Farce, that most exhilarating theatrical form, has been a favorite of the light dramatic palette since the Middle Ages, when brief comic pieces were stuffed ("farce" being derived from a culinary form for "stuffing") between long, usually ponderous, heavy courses of a more tragic character. From the same nation that invented sorbet, come the quintessential "digestive comedy," in the form of vintage French farce.

LAIS:	THE POOR BEGGAR AND THE FAIRY GODMOTHER
OURTELINE:	BOUBOUROCHE, or SHE DUPES TO CONQUER
YDEAU:	A FITTING CONFUSION; A FLEA IN HER REAR, or ANTS IN HER PANTS; GOING TO POT
ABICHE:	IT'S ALL RELATIVE
EILHAC AND HALÉVY:	MARDI GRAS; SIGNOR NICODEMO
ARDOU:	FOR LOVE OR MONKEY

Shapiro writes well about the edge of madness that Feydeau's characters are always so perilously skirting...His versions read easily. It is a greater achievement that [the plays] seem actable."

—Times Literary Supplement

ISBN: 1-55783-165-3 $15.95 paper

THE REDUCED SHAKESPEARE COMPANY'S
COMPLEAT WORKS OF
WLLM SHKSPR

by Jess Borgeson, Adam Long and Daniel Singer

"ABSL HLRS."

> – THE INDEPENDENT (LONDON)

"SHAKESPEARE WRIT SMALL, AS YOU MIGHT LIKE IT!...PITHIER-THAN-PYTHON PARODIES... NOT TO BE CONFUSED WITH THAT AUGUST ENGLISH COMPANY WITH THE SAME INITIALS. THIS ICONOCLASTIC AMERICAN TROUPE DOES MORE WITH LESS."

> – THE NEW YORK TIMES

"STUPENDOUS, ANCHORLESS JOY!"

> – BERNARD LEVIN
> THE NEW YORK TIMES

"SHAKESPEARE AS WRITTEN BY *READER'S DIGEST*, ACTED BY MONTY PYTHON, AND PER-FORMED AT THE SPEED OF THE MINUTE WALTZ. SO FORSOOTH! GET THEE TO THE RSC'S DELIGHTFULLY FRACTURED COMPLETE WORKS."

> – LOS ANGELES HERALD

ISBN: 1-55783-157-2 $8.95 paper